KS3 HISTORY

Third Edition

Renaissance, Revolution and Reformation

Britain 1509–1745

Aaron Wilkes
Ellen Longley

Teacher Handbook

OXFORD
UNIVERSITY PRESS

UNIVERSITY PRESS

Great Clarendon Street, Oxford, OX2 6DP, United Kingdom

Oxford University Press is a department of the University of Oxford.
It furthers the University's objective of excellence in research, scholarship,
and education by publishing worldwide. Oxford is a registered trade mark of
Oxford University Press in the UK and in
certain other countries

© Oxford University Press 2014

The moral rights of the authors have been asserted

First published in 2014

British Library Cataloguing in Publication Data
Data available

978-0-19-839324-5

10 9 8 7 6 5 4 3 2 1

Paper used in the production of this book is a natural, recyclable product
made from wood grown in sustainable forests.
The manufacturing process conforms to the environmental regulations of
the country of origin.

Printed in Great Britain by Ashford Print and Publishing Services,
Gosport.

Acknowledgements
Cover illustration by Matthew Hollings

Although we have made every effort to trace and contact all
copyright holders before publication this has not been possible in all
cases. If notified, the publisher will rectify any errors or omissions at
the earliest opportunity.

From the author, Ellen Longley: With love and thanks to my
fantastic husband and parents who support me without question
in everything I do. And my daughters, Jess and Beth, who make me
proud every day.

Links to third party websites are provided by Oxford in good faith
and for information only. Oxford disclaims any responsibility for
the materials contained in any third party website referenced in
this work.

Contents

Scheme of work

This table shows all the lessons available in the *Renaissance, Revolution and Reformation Student Book*, in the *Key Stage 3 History* series, so that you can easily navigate through the book and supporting digital material on Kerboodle to select the key themes and topics that you might use to inform your own scheme of work.

Key to resources

SB – Student Book

TH – Teacher Handbook

K – Kerboodle

Lesson title	Key Question	Resources
A journey through time from 1509 to 1745	What will we be learning in History this year?	• SB pp.6–7
Chapter 1: Here come the Tudors		**1 Source Bank, 1 Auto-Marked Test on Kerboodle**
1.1A What was Britain like in 1509?	What was Britain's relationship with its neighbouring countries like in 1509?	• SB pp.8–9 • TH p.24 • K 1.1A Enquiry History Skills Activity • K 1.1A Changes Worksheet 1 • K 1.1A Changes Worksheet 2
1.1B What was Britain like in 1509?	What was everyday life like in 1509?	• SB pp.10–11 • TH p.25 • K 1.1B Enquiry History Skills Activity • K 1.1B Fete Worksheet
1.2 What was young Henry VIII like?	How did young Henry VIII spend his time and money?	• SB pp.12–13 • TH p.26 • K 1.2 Using Evidence History Skills Activity • K 1.2 Young Henry VIII Worksheet 1 • K 1.2 Young Henry VIII Worksheet 2
1.3 Henry VIII, his first wife and his big problem	How did Henry falling out with the Pope affect religion in England?	• SB pp.14–15 • TH p.27 • K 1.3 Cause and Consequence History Skills Activity • K 1.3 Cartoon Strip Worksheet • K 1.3 Wives Mini-Movie
1.4 Who'd want to marry King Henry VIII?	What happened to each of Henry's six wives?	• SB pp.16–17 • TH p.28 • K 1.4 Significance History Skills Activity • K 1.4 Advice Worksheet • K 1.4 Katherine Film Clip • K 1.4 Film Worksheet
1.5 What did Protestants protest about?	What was the difference between a Catholic and a Protestant?	• SB pp.18–20 • TH p.29 • K 1.5 Using Evidence History Skills Activity • K 1.5 Poster Worksheet
1.6 History Mystery: Why did the *Mary Rose* sink?	What can evidence tell us about how the *Mary Rose* sank?	• SB pp.20–21 • TH p.30 • K 1.6 Using Evidence History Skills Activity • K 1.6 Plaque Worksheet • K 1.6 Sailor Film Clip • K 1.6 Film Worksheet
1.7 Edward VI: the boy king	How did Edward VI change religion in England?	• SB pp.22–23 • TH p.31 • K 1.7 Change and Continuity History Skills Activity • K 1.7 Obituary Worksheet • K 1.7 Churches Mini-Movie
1.8 How bloody was Bloody Mary?	How did Bloody Mary get her nickname and did she deserve it?	• SB pp.24–25 • TH p.32 • K 1.8 Using Evidence History Skills Activity • K 1.8 Nasty Nickname Worksheet
1.9 The nastiest nursery rhyme in the world!	What is the hidden meaning of the nursery rhyme, 'Mary, Mary, quite contrary'?	• SB pp.26–27 • TH p.33 • K 1.9 Interpretations History Skills Activity • K 1.9 Nursery Rhyme Worksheet
1.10 Elizabeth's middle way	How did Elizabeth I try to end religious turmoil in Tudor England?	• SB pp.28–29 • TH p.34 • K 1.10 Understanding Diversity History Skills Activity • K 1.10 Compromise Worksheet
Assessing Your Learning 1	Who was the most successful Tudor monarch?	• SB pp.30–33 • TH pp.35–36 • K Assessment Task Presentation 1 • K Assessment Worksheet 1 • K Success Criteria Teacher Grid 1

Chapter 2: A world of discovery		2 Source Bank, 2 Auto-Marked Test on Kerboodle
2.1 The man who wanted to know everything	What made Leonardo da Vinci such an important 'Renaissance man'?	· SB pp.34–35 · TH p.39 · K 2.1 Significance History Skills Activity · K 2.1 Renaissance Worksheet 1 · K 2.1 Renaissance Worksheet 2 · K 2.1 Leonardo Film Clip · K 2.1 Film Worksheet
2.2A Exploring the world	Why were Renaissance explorers so keen to find new routes to foreign lands?	· SB pp.36–37 · TH p.40 · K 2.2A Using Evidence History Skills Activity · K 2.2A Known World Worksheet
2.2B Exploring the world	Who were the most significant Renaissance explorers?	· SB pp.38–39 · TH p.41 · K 2.2B Significance History Skills Activity · K 2.2B Discovery Worksheet · K 2.2B Columbus Film Clip · K 2.2B Film Worksheet · K 2.2B Explorers Mini-Movie
Chapter 3: Life in Tudor times		**3 Source Bank, 3 Auto-Marked Test on Kerboodle**
3.1A Who's who?	What four main groups made up Tudor society?	· SB pp.40–41 · TH p.44 · K 3.1A Understanding Diversity History Skills Activity · K 3.1A Class Worksheet
3.1B Who's who?	How were paupers dealt with?	· SB pp.42–43 · TH p.45 · K 3.1B Understanding Diversity History Skills Activity · K 3.1B Paupers Worksheet
3.2 What were Tudor schools like?	How do Tudor schools compare with modern schools?	· SB pp.44–45 · TH p.46 · K 3.2 Change and Continuity History Skills Activity · K 3.2 School Diary Worksheet · K 3.2 Teacher Film Clip · K 3.2 Film Worksheet
3.3A How did people have fun in Tudor times?	What kind of activities did Tudor people enjoy?	· SB pp.46–47 · TH p.47 · K 3.3A Change and Continuity History Skills Activity · K 3.3A Entertainment Worksheet
3.3B How did people have fun in Tudor times?	How did ordinary people spend their free time?	· SB pp.48–49 · TH p.48 · K 3.3B Using Evidence History Skills Activity · K 3.3B Fun and Games Worksheet 1 · K 3.3B Fun and Games Worksheet 2
3.4 And now for your Shakespeare lesson…	Why did William Shakespeare become the most famous Englishman in the world?	· SB pp.50–51 · TH p.49 · K 3.4 Using Evidence History Skills Activity · K 3.4 Advert Worksheet
3.5 Shakespeare or Fakespeare?	Who actually wrote the works of Shakespeare?	· SB pp.52–53 · TH p.50 · K 3.5 Using Evidence History Skills Activity · K 3.5 Real or Fake? Worksheet
3.6 Fashion victims	What did rich Tudor women do to their faces and why?	· SB pp.54–55 · TH p.51 · K 3.6 Using Evidence History Skills Activity · K 3.6 Matching Worksheet
3.7 Come dine with me!	How does our modern daily routine differ from that of people in Tudor times?	· SB pp.56–57 · TH p.52 · K 3.7 Using Evidence History Skills Activity · K 3.7 Etiquette Worksheet · K 3.7 Country Life Film Clip · K 3.7 Film Worksheet
3.8A Crimewatch	How did poorer people try to make money in Tudor times?	· SB pp.58–59 · TH p.53 · K 3.8A Cause and Consequence History Skills Activity · K 3.8A Tricksters Worksheet
3.8B Crimewatch	How did Tudor society deal with the poor?	· SB pp.60–61 · TH p.54 · K 3.8B Chronology History Skills Activity · K 3.8B Using Evidence History Skills Activity · K 3.8B Conviction Worksheet
3.9 What did the Scottish boot, the Judas cradle and the Spanish donkey have in common?	What tortures were used during the Tudor and Stuart periods and why?	· SB pp.62–63 · TH p.55 · K 3.9 Interpretations History Skills Activity · K 3.9 Notes Worksheet · K 3.9 Tower Film Clip · K 3.9 Film Worksheet

Chapter 4: Britain abroad		4 Source Bank, 4 Auto-Marked Test on Kerboodle
4.1A How did Britain build an empire?	How and why did the British Empire begin?	• SB pp.64–65 • TH p.58 • K 4.1A Cause and Consequence History Skills Activity • K 4.1A Great Explorers Worksheet 1 • K 4.1A Great Explorers Worksheet 2
4.1B How did Britain build an empire?	Who were the significant individuals in the growth of the British Empire?	• SB pp.66–67 • TH p.59 • K 4.1B Using Evidence History Skills Activity • K 4.1B Trade Worksheet • K 4.1B Company Film Clip • K 4.1B Film Worksheet
4.2 How was Britain involved in the slave trade?	Why did British traders take slaves to the New World?	• SB pp.68–69 • TH p.60 • K 4.2 Using Evidence History Skills Activity • K 4.2 Slavery Worksheet 1 • K 4.2 Slavery Worksheet 2 • K 4.2 Trader Film Clip • K 4.2 Film Worksheet • K 4.2 Slave Triangle Mini-Movie
4.3 Blackbeard: the original pirate of the Caribbean	How did pirates differ from privateers?	• SB pp.70–71 • TH p.61 • K 4.3 Interpretations History Skills Activity • K 4.3 Pirates Worksheet 1 • K 4.3 Pirates Worksheet 2 • K 4.3 Edward Teach Film Clip • K 4.3 Film Worksheet
Chapter 5: Queen Elizabeth		5 Source Bank, 5 Auto-Marked Test on Kerboodle
5.1 Young Elizabeth: what was she like?	How clever was young Elizabeth and how did she become queen?	• SB pp.72–73 • TH p.64 • K 5.1 Using Evidence History Skills Activity • K 5.1 School Report Worksheet
5.2 What did Queen Elizabeth look like?	Why did Elizabeth control her royal portraits so carefully?	• SB pp.74–75 • TH p.65 • K 5.2 Using Evidence History Skills Activity • K 5.2 Paintings Worksheet 1 • K 5.2 Paintings Worksheet 2 • K 5.2 Rainbow Portrait Mini-Movie
5.3 Why did Queen Elizabeth kill her cousin?	What threat did Mary, Queen of Scots, pose to Elizabeth?	• SB pp.76–77 • TH p.66 • K 5.3 Enquiry History Skills Activity • K 5.3 Elizabeth and Mary Worksheet 1 • K 5.3 Elizabeth and Mary Worksheet 2
5.4A Match of the day: England versus Spain	Why did the King of Spain decide to invade England in 1588?	• SB pp.78–79 • TH p.67 • K 5.4A Cause and Consequence History Skills Activity • K 5.4A Ships Worksheet • K 5.4A Cannons Film Clip • K 5.4A Film Worksheet
5.4B Match of the day: England versus Spain	Why did the Spanish Armada fail?	• SB pp.80–81 • TH p.68 • K 5.4B Using Evidence History Skills Activity • K 5.4B Spanish Armada Worksheet 1 • K 5.4B Spanish Armada Worksheet 2
Assessing Your Learning 2	What symbolism can be found in the Rainbow Portrait?	• SB pp.82–83 • TH pp.69–70 • K Assessment Task Presentation 2 • K Assessment Worksheet 2 • K Success Criteria Teacher Grid 2
Chapter 6: Exit the Tudors, enter the Stuarts		6 Source Bank, 6 Auto-Marked Test on Kerboodle
6.1 The scruffy Stuart!	Why did the English throne pass to the Scottish royal family?	• SB pp.84–85 • TH p.73 • K 6.1 Using Evidence History Skills Activity • K 6.1 Interpretations History Skills Activity • K 6.1 England and Scotland Worksheet 1 • K 6.1 England and Scotland Worksheet 2
6.2 Remember, remember the fifth of November!	What role did key individuals play in the Gunpowder Plot?	• SB pp.86–87 • TH p.74 • K 6.2 Using Evidence History Skills Activity • K 6.2 Letter Worksheet • K 6.2 Mystery Film Clip • K 6.2 Film Worksheet • K 6.2 Execution Mini-Movie
6.3 History Mystery: Were the gunpowder plotters framed?	What evidence suggests the gunpowder plotters might have been framed?	• SB pp.88–89 • TH p.75 • K 6.3 Enquiry History Skills Activity • K 6.3 Report Worksheet

6.4 Which witch is which?	Who might have been accused of witchcraft in Stuart times?	• SB pp.90–91 • TH p.76 • K 6.4 Using Evidence History Skills Activity • K 6.4 Witch-Hunt Worksheet • K 6.4 Dungeon Film Clip • K 6.4 Film Worksheet
6.5A Why do Americans speak English?	Why and how did the English start to settle in North America?	• SB pp.92–93 • TH p77 • K 6.5A Significance History Skills Activity • K 6.5A Puritans Worksheet
6.5B Why do Americans speak English?	What happened to the early English colonies in North America?	• SB pp.94–95 • TH p.78 • K 6.5B Chronology History Skills Activity • K 6.5B Settlers Worksheet 1 • K 6.5B Settlers Worksheet 2

Chapter 7: England at war	**7 Source Bank, 7 Auto-Marked Test on Kerboodle**	
7.1 Why did the English start fighting each other?	What is a civil war and how did England's start?	• SB pp.96–97 • TH p.81 • K 7.1 Cause and Consequence History Skills Activity • K 7.1 Civil War Worksheet
7.2 Match of the day: Roundheads versus Cavaliers	How did soldiers fight in the Civil War and what did they look like?	• SB pp.98–99 • TH p.82 • K 7.2 Enquiry History Skills Activity • K 7.2 Soldiers Worksheet 1 • K 7.2 Soldiers Worksheet 2 • K 7.2 Brothers Film Clip • K 7.2 Film Worksheet
7.3 Prince Rupert: mad Cavalier or sad Cavalier?	Who was Prince Rupert and why was he so popular with Royalists?	• SB pp.100–101 • TH p.83 • K 7.3 Using Evidence History Skills Activity • K 7.3 Prince Rupert Worksheet 1 • K 7.3 Prince Rupert Worksheet 2
7.4 What was new about the New Model Army?	What made the New Model Army such an effective fighting force?	• SB pp.102–103 • TH p.84 • K 7.4 Using Evidence History Skills Activity • K 7.4 Speech Worksheet • K 7.4 Musketeer Film Clip • K 7.4 Film Worksheet
7.5A Why was King Charles I sentenced to death?	How and why was King Charles I put on trial?	• SB pp.104–105 • TH p.85 • K 7.5A Using Evidence History Skills Activity • K 7.5A Charles I Worksheet 1 • K 7.5A Charles I Worksheet 2
7.5B Why was King Charles I sentenced to death?	How did the judges at Charles I's trial arrive at their verdict?	• SB pp.106–107 • TH p.86 • K 7.5B Enquiry History Skills Activity • K 7.5B Trial Worksheet
7.6 Charlie for the chop!	What's so significant about 30 January 1649?	• SB pp.108–109 • TH p.87 • K 7.6 Using Evidence History Skills Activity • K 7.6 Journalism Worksheet 1 • K 7.6 Journalism Worksheet 2

Chapter 8: Cromwell's Commonwealth	**8 Source Bank, 8 Auto-Marked Test on Kerboodle**	
8.1 The man who banned Christmas	How did the country change under Cromwell?	• SB pp.110–111 • TH p.90 • K 8.1 Significance History Skills Activity • K 8.1 Interregnum Worksheet 1 • K 8.1 Interregnum Worksheet 2
8.2 Cromwell: curse of Ireland?	What did Cromwell do to earn his reputation in Ireland and does he deserve it?	• SB pp.112–113 • TH p.91 • K 8.2 Using Evidence History Skills Activity • K 8.2 Cromwell Worksheet 1 • K 8.2 Cromwell Worksheet 2 • K 8.2 Drogheda Mini-Movie
8.3 Cromwell: hero or villain?	Should Cromwell be seen as a hero or a villain?	• SB pp.114–115 • TH p.92 • K 8.3 Using Evidence History Skills Activity • K 8.3 Decision Worksheet • K 8.3 Interview Film Clip • K 8.3 Film Worksheet
8.4A Whatever happened to Cromwell's head?	How did England become a monarchy once more?	• SB pp.116–117 • TH p.93 • K 8.4A Chronology History Skills Activity • K 8.4A Storyboard Worksheet
8.4B Whatever happened to Cromwell's head?	How did King Charles II seek revenge after 1660?	• SB pp.118–119 • TH p.94 • K 8.4B Chronology History Skills Activity • K 8.4B Story Worksheet

Chapter 9: The Restoration		9 Source Bank, 9 Auto-Marked Test on Kerboodle
9.1 Who was the Merry Monarch?	How did Charles II become king and how was his nation different from Cromwell's?	• SB pp.120–121 • TH p.97 • K 9.1 Significance History Skills Activity • K 9.1 Charles II Worksheet 1 • K 9.1 Charles II Worksheet 2
9.2 Bring out your dead!	What did people know about the spread of plague and disease in seventeenth-century London?	• SB pp.122–123 • TH p.98 • K 9.2 Using Evidence History Skills Activity • K 9.2 Plague Worksheet
9.3 Ring a ring o' roses	How does a nursery rhyme tell us how people tried to avoid catching the plague?	• SB pp.124–125 • TH p.99 • K 9.3 Cause and Consequence History Skills Activity • K 9.3 Symptoms Worksheet 1 • K 9.3 Symptoms Worksheet 2
9.4A Who started the Great Fire of London?	How did the Great Fire devastate London?	• SB pp.126–127 • TH p.100 • K 9.4A Using Evidence History Skills Activity • K 9.4A Story Worksheet • K 9.4A Aftermath Film Clip • K 9.4A Film Worksheet
9.4B Who started the Great Fire of London?	How and why have interpretations of the cause of the Great Fire changed since 1666?	• SB pp.128–129 • TH p.101 • K 9.4B Cause and Consequence History Skills Activity • K 9.4B Fire! Worksheet 1 • K 9.4B Fire! Worksheet 2
9.4C Who started the Great Fire of London?	How was London rebuilt after 1666?	• SB pp.130–131 • TH p.102 • K 9.4C Cause and Consequence History Skills Activity • K 9.4C Rebuilding Worksheet 1 • K 9.4C Rebuilding Worksheet 2
9.5 What about the women?	How were rich and poor women treated in Tudor and Stuart times?	• SB pp.132–133 • TH p.103 • K 9.5 Using Evidence History Skills Activity • K 9.5 Women Worksheet • K 9.5 Daily Life Film Clip • K 9.5 Film Worksheet
9.6 Can you cure King Charles II?	What kind of treatments were on offer to King Charles II?	• SB pp.134–135 • TH p.104 • K 9.6 Enquiry History Skills Activity • K 9.6 Diagnosis Worksheet 1 • K 9.6 Diagnosis Worksheet 2
Chapter 10: Who rules?		11 Source Bank, 11 Auto-Marked Test on Kerboodle
10.1A The Glorious Revolution	How and why did the monarchy change?	• SB pp.136–137 • TH p.107 • K 10.1A Cause and Consequence History Skills Activity • K 10.1A Revolution Worksheet 1 • K 10.1A Revolution Worksheet 2
10.1B The Glorious Revolution	What changes did William and Mary agree to?	• SB pp.138–139 • TH p.108 • K 10.1B Using Evidence History Skills Activity • K 10.1B Bill of Rights Worksheet
10.2 Exit the Stuarts… enter the Georgians	How was the United Kingdom established?	• SB pp.140–141 • TH p.109 • K 10.2 Understanding Diversity History Skills Activity • K 10.2 Timeline Worksheet
10.3 The Battle of Culloden	Why was Bonnie Prince Charlie a threat to the Georgians?	• SB pp.142–143 • TH p.110 • K 10.3 Using Evidence History Skills Activity • K 10.3 Jacobites Worksheet • K 10.3 Conflict Film Clip • K 10.3 Film Worksheet

Chapter 11: How did Britain change?		10 Source Bank, 10 Auto-Marked Test on Kerboodle
11.1A What does Robert know that John didn't?	What were the key discoveries, theories and inventions of the sixteenth, seventeenth and early eighteenth centuries?	• SB pp.144–145 • TH p.113 • K 11.1A Using Evidence History Skills Activity • K 11.1A Science Worksheet
11.1B What does Robert know that John didn't?	What was the difference between the Age of Faith and the Age of Reason?	• SB pp.146–147 • TH p.114 • K 11.1B Using Evidence History Skills Activity • K 11.1B Robert Worksheet • K 11.1B John and Robert Film Clip • K 11.1B Film Worksheet
11.2A A changing nation	How far did Britain change between 1509 and 1745?	• SB pp.148–149 • TH p.115 • K 11.2A Change and Continuity History Skills Activity • K 11.2A Advertisement Worksheet
11.2B A changing nation	What important ideas and inventions came from this time?	• SB pp.150–151 • TH p.116 • K 11.2B Change and Continuity History Skills Activity • K 11.2B Significance History Skills Activity • K 11.2B Changing Britain Worksheet
Assessing Your Learning 3	Which individual from this period is the most significant?	• SB pp.152–153 • TH pp.117–118 • K Assessment Task Presentation 3 • K Assessment Worksheet 3 • K Success Criteria Teacher Grid 3

Introduction

A unique approach

The *KS3 History* series by Aaron Wilkes has become one of the best-selling secondary school History series in recent years. This is its Third Edition, published in line with the new National Curriculum for 2014.

KS3 History is not just a series of textbooks. The materials which accompany them make up a complete scheme of work for a comprehensive Key Stage 3 History course. However, the scheme is not meant to be prescriptive. Experienced teachers may want to plunder the materials for suitable resources and ideas, whilst supply teachers, non-specialists or those just starting out in the profession will soon realise that *KS3 History* is a proven scheme of work that has proven effective with the students in the classroom.

The series itself sticks rigidly to the idea that any resources used with students should be as entertaining, accessible and relevant as possible because children learn best when they are interested and engaged in activities that they think are both challenging and worthwhile. If a group of students are hooked early on in a lesson by a disgusting picture, a curious title or a thought-provoking objective, a highly proactive learning environment can be created. Each topic in the book aims to get the students involved, and keep them involved, through imaginatively presented double-page spreads with a clear route through them, headed by progressive learning objectives and finished off with a work section that aims to make the written part of any lesson as much fun and as challenging as possible. Great emphasis has been placed on designing tasks and activities that help students understand the key concepts relating to the study of History and develop the skills needed to become a top historian.

The *Student Books* contain quirky facts, extension and assessment opportunities, and the correct historical vocabulary. The *Kerboodle Lessons, Resources and Assessment* material provides starters, summative and formative assessment opportunities, customizable worksheets, interactive activities, lesson plans, and short films on the key topics.

Developing Skills

In recent years, greater emphasis has been placed on developing students' chronological understanding. *KS3 History* provides an effective base from which to do this throughout the whole of Key Stage 3. The books are written in chronological order, starting in the medieval period and going through to the twenty-first century. With each book and accompanying Kerboodle package, students are encouraged to develop their understanding of the relevant historical conventions by using precise dates, correct vocabulary and chronological terms. A student's sense of chronology, sequence and duration is developed through the use of overviews, summative tasks, enquiry-based topics and concept-specific work sections.

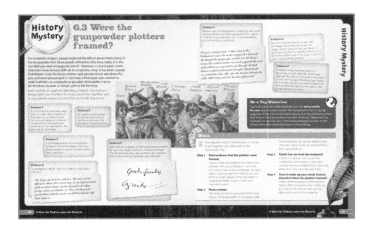

The series also provides a stimulating backdrop for promoting students' knowledge, encouraging their communication skills and their understanding of historical evidence. Some topics, such as *6.3 Were the gunpowder plotters framed?*, are presented as a History Mystery for students to weigh evidence and analyse sources. They are required to use strategies and enquiry techniques to arrive at effective and reasoned conclusions. In each book, there are specific spreads that are designed to help students develop insights into values, beliefs and culture as well as encouraging their understanding of key processes. For example, in *Chapter 4 Britain abroad* and *6.5 Why do Americans speak English?* students will consider how Britain has influenced, and been influenced by, the wider world, while in *Chapter 3 Life in Tudor Times* they will explore concepts such as change and continuity and similarity and difference. Further, in *Chapter 10 Who rules?* students are required to analyse the short- and long-term consequences of the Glorious Revolution and

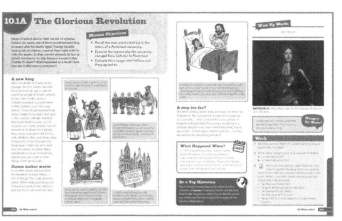

will make connections to Britain's system of parliamentary democracy today. In *8.3 Cromwell: hero or villain?* students are asked to discern how Cromwell has been interpreted and why, while the Assessing Your Learning challenges encourage them to investigate historical concepts such as significance, and require them to justify their opinions, interrogate sources, make connections, and draw contrasts. The skills are mapped by lesson onto grids in this book e.g. page 22.

Literacy in History

Each spread contains a small selection of vital 'Wise Up Words'. Students should be encouraged to look up their meanings in a dictionary and/or use the glossary and index at the back of the book. They should be able to spell, understand and use the words correctly, and the tasks will ask the students to define and deploy these words with precision.

Students are asked to cover basic literacy competencies in the Work sections. They are instructed to 'write in full sentences', 'use capital letters and full stops', and back up their views 'with evidence from the sources'. They are taught to construct a proper paragraph, make a point, 'evidence it', and explain what they mean in preparation for GCSE. There is also a range of activities that employ a variety of creative literacy strategies.

kerboodle

Renaissance, Revolution and Reformation: Britain 1509–1745 Kerboodle Lessons, Resources and Assessment provides hundreds of lively digital resources, including:

- unique specially commissioned films from The History Squad and film worksheets
- History skills activities
- source banks/collections
- worksheets and self-assessments
- ready-to-go lesson presentations
- supported assessment tasks with success criteria and marking guidance.

You can adapt many of these resources to suit you and your students' individual needs and upload your existing resources so everything can be accessed from one location to help bring History to life in your classroom.

Assessment and progression

Each book, and its accompanying Kerboodle package, includes a ready-made set of formative and summative assessment tasks.

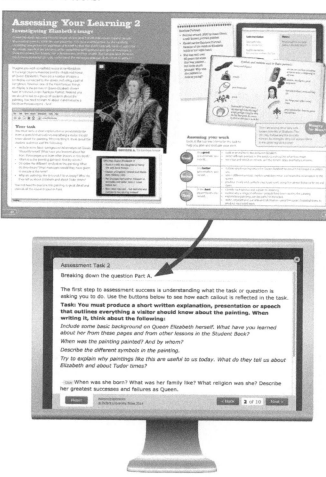

- Learning objectives for each spread are written in student-friendly language. These can be referred to easily throughout any lesson.
- In 'Assessing Your Learning' sections within each book, students' understanding of skills and concepts is tested. Students are made aware of the standards they are aiming for, using the 'good, better, best' model.
- The assessment support package on *Kerboodle* includes: step-by-step task presentations for front-of-class use, self- and peer-assessment worksheets, and auto-marked tests.

We sincerely hope that *KS3 History* helps you deliver the outstanding lessons that we all aspire to, and that the history package we've developed helps inspire and engage a new generation of learners.

With best wishes

Aaron Wilkes   Ellen Longley

About this series

Renaissance, Revolution and Reformation: Britain 1509–1745 is one of four Third Edition *Student Books* in the popular **Key Stage 3 History** series by experienced Head of History, Aaron Wilkes.

Written to match the 2014 National Curriculum, this series uses a fresh angle on great stories in history to hook students' interest in Key Stage 3 History whilst preparing them for GCSE.

On Kerboodle, films from British Pathé and the History Squad and other exciting multimedia resources are fully integrated with the *Student Books* and *Teacher Handbooks*, so your lessons can be delivered easily and seamlessly, containing plenty to help you stir, challenge and inspire your young historians!

The series components

The series consists of:

For students
- Four *Student Books* (and/or four *Kerboodle Books*)
- Four Kerboodle *Lessons, Resources and Assessments*.

For teachers
- Four *Teacher Handbooks*
- Four Kerboodle *Lessons, Resources and Assessment* packages (includes teacher access to the accompanying *Kerboodle Book*).

Student Book

The **Key Stage 3 History: Renaissance, Revolution and Reformation: Britain 1509–1745 Student Book** uses an entertaining narrative to hook interest and make stories memorable. Throughout the book, lessons and tasks are designed to develop key skills and processes and understand historical terms and concepts, including making connections.

Key to icons

Source bank | Film | Worksheet | History skills activity | Literacy | Numeracy

---

Wise Up Words
The important phrases and terms are highlighted. Emphasis should be placed on getting the students to learn how to spell and use these words and phrases correctly.

Mission Objectives
All sections start by setting the students some 'Mission Objectives'. Generally speaking, they are progressive, which means they often begin with a lower order concept such as comprehension or application (define, recall, relate, identify etc.) leading to higher order concepts such as analysis and evaluation (justify, assess, judge, predict etc.).

Fact!
Funny, fascinating and amazing little stories and snippets of history are dotted throughout the books. They are often the piece of information in the spread that gest most student reaction!

Work
The tasks in the Work section aim to develop the key skills and concepts that all good History students should focus on. Generally speaking, the tasks are progressive in terms of difficulty and there is often a 'creative' element to one or more of the tasks. The tasks in the Work section also encourage students to develop all sorts of literacy skills relating to speaking, listening, reading and writing. They are often asked to use writing as a tool for their thoughts and encouraged to record, develop and evaluate their ideas as well as read for meaning and complete tasks related to the text in the spread.

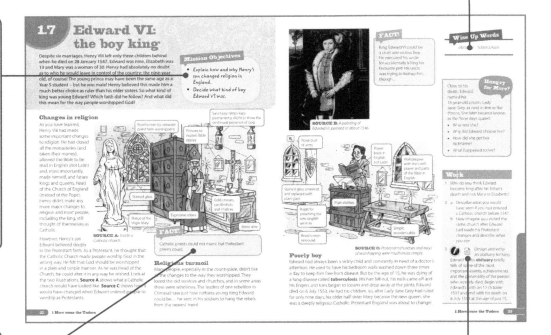

Depth Study

In each book, there is a mini depth study that focuses in more detail on an important and significant event or concept of the period. These sections give students the chance to extend and deepen their understanding of key moments in history.

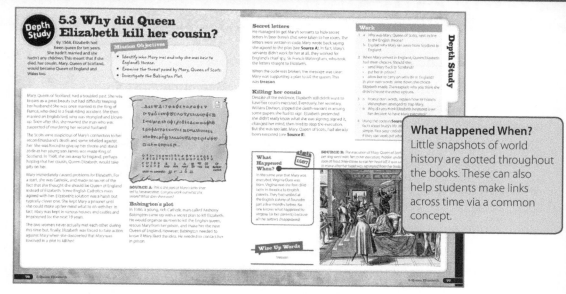

What Happened When?
Little snapshots of world history are dotted throughout the books. These can also help students make links across time via a common concept.

History Mystery

Some of the period's more intriguing, interesting or more controversial topics are covered as History Mystery. A step-by-step approach is used so students can evaluate evidence, consider interpretations and come to their own conclusions.

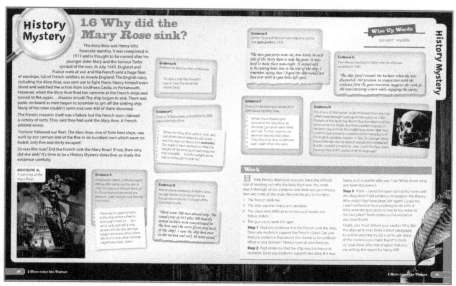

Assessing Your Learning

In the book, there are three extended assessments. These are opportunities for students to showcase what they have learned about the topic and assess their research and analysis skills. Some are more creative, while others will focus on extended writing or looking at sources. Full marking support is provided in this handbook and on Kerboodle.

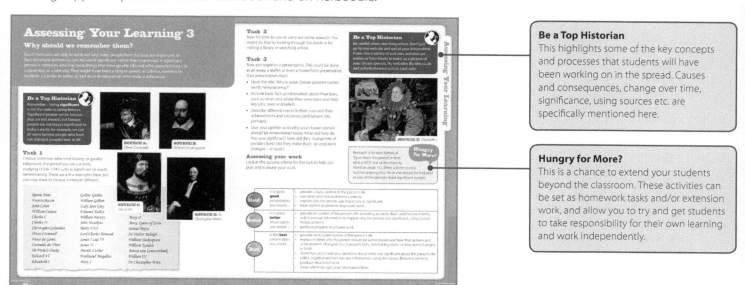

Be a Top Historian
This highlights some of the key concepts and processes that students will have been working on in the spread. Causes and consequences, change over time, significance, using sources etc. are specifically mentioned here.

Hungry for More?
This is a chance to extend your students beyond the classroom. These activities can be set as homework tasks and/or extension work, and allow you to try and get students to take responsibility for their own learning and work independently.

Using this book

Teacher Handbook

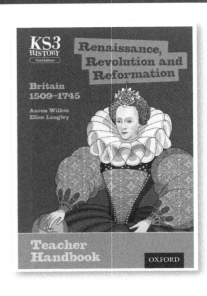

The *Key Stage 3 History: Renaissance, Revolution and Reformation: Britain 1509–1745 Teacher Handbook* aims to save you time and effort! It provides **full support** and guidance for the *Renaissance, Revolution and Reformation: Britain 1509–1745 Student Book*, including **practical tasks**, an **assessment package** and **creative suggestions** for incorporating differentiation into your teaching.

What it provides
Closely matched to each chapter of the *Student Book*, this book provides:

1 a chapter overview
2 help at a glance for each double-page spread in the *Student Book*
3 further suggestions for starters, plenaries and differentiation
4 an assessment overview.

Please turn to the **Contents List** on page 3 to see how this book is structured.
A Scheme of Work is also provided on pages 4–9 to help you select the key themes and topics that you might use to inform your own planning.

Find out more about the four main components below.

1 The chapter overview
This is your introduction to the corresponding *Student Book* chapter.

- Shows how the *Student Book* chapter relates to the 2014 National Curriculum

- Sets out the key ideas and skills development within the chapter in the *Student Book*

- Sets out the objectives and outcomes for the chapter, and the corresponding lesson numbers

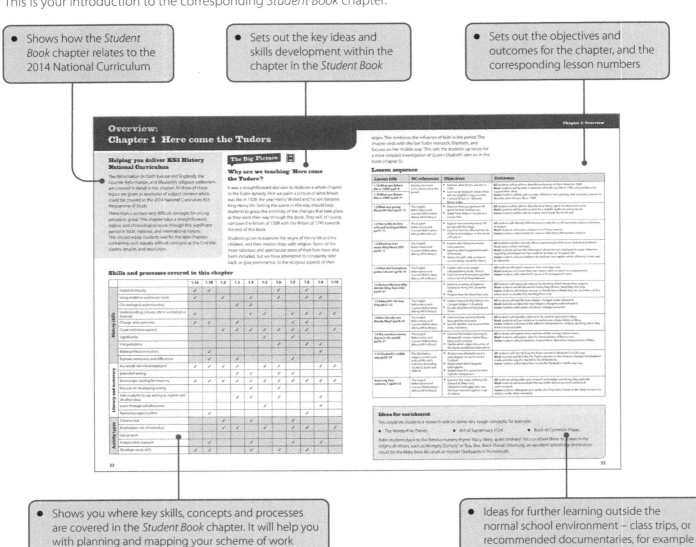

- Shows you where key skills, concepts and processes are covered in the *Student Book* chapter. It will help you with planning and mapping your scheme of work

- Ideas for further learning outside the normal school environment – class trips, or recommended documentaries, for example

2 Help at a glance for each lesson

These pages give comprehensive help for each lesson in the *Renaissance, Revolution and Reformation: Britain 1509–1745 Student Book*.

- Starts with a brief walk through the lesson, to show you how it develops and what the expected outcomes are

- A list of all the resources available on Kerboodle for the lesson

- This section provides clarification and extra information for some activities in the *Student Book*, and potential assessment opportunities

- Offers alternative activities and suggestions to support and extend your students

- Suggestion for a possible starter

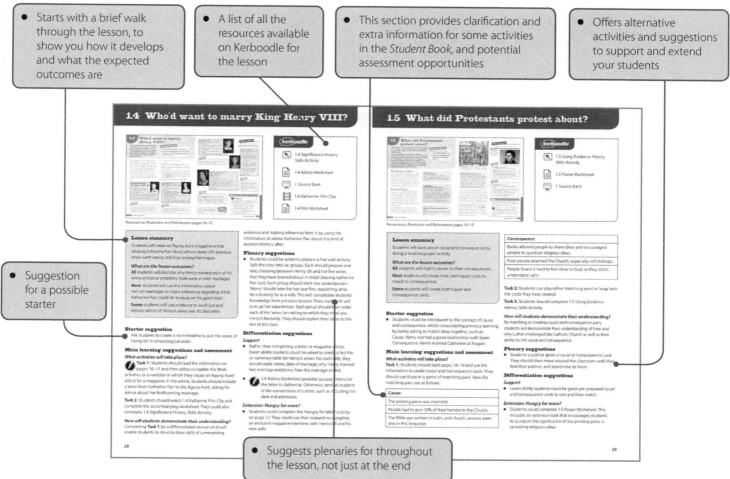

- Suggests plenaries for throughout the lesson, not just at the end

Assessment

This section introduces you to the end-of-chapter assessment task from the *Student Book*, and describes the support materials available for the chapter.

- You can see all the assessment materials available for the chapter at a glance

- The purpose of the assessment task from the *Student Book* is summarized

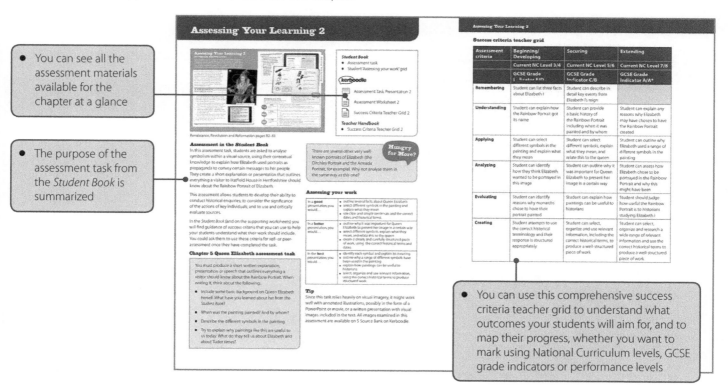

- You can use this comprehensive success criteria teacher grid to understand what outcomes your students will aim for, and to map their progress, whether you want to mark using National Curriculum levels, GCSE grade indicators or performance levels

Kerboodle

Key Stage 3 Renaissance, Revolution and Reformation: Britain 1509–1745 Kerboodle is packed full of guided support and ideas for running and creating effective History lessons. It's intuitive to use, customizable, and can be accessed online.

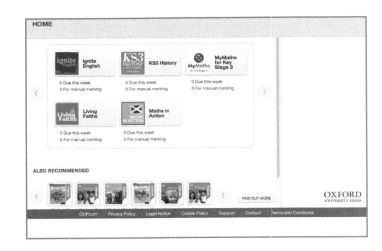

Kerboodle consists of:

- *Lessons, Resources and Assessment* (includes teacher access to the accompanying *Kerboodle Book*) for *Renaissance, Revolution and Reformation: Britain 1509–1745*
- *Renaissance, Revolution and Reformation: Britain 1509–1745 Kerboodle Book*.

Lessons, Resources and Assessment

Renaissance, Revolution and Reformation: Britain 1509–1745 Kerboodle Lessons, Resources and Assessment provides hundreds of lively built-in resources, including unique specially commissioned films from The History Squad, interactive activities, ready-to-go lesson presentations, and supported assessment tasks with success criteria and marking guidance. You can **adapt** many of these resources to suit you and your students' individual needs, and **upload** your existing resources so everything can be accessed from one location. Image collections are also included to help bring History to life in your classroom.

Lessons, Resources and Assessment provides:

1 Resources   3 Assessment and Markbook
2 Lessons   4 Teacher access to the *Kerboodle Book*.

Find out more about the four main components below.

Resources

Click on the **Resources** tab at the top of the screen to access the full list of resources for *Renaissance, Revolution and Reformation: Britain 1509–1745*.

- You can bring in many of your own resources by clicking the Upload button

- Find all the resources associated with every *Student Book* chapter or lesson

- Click here to launch the corresponding *Kerboodle Book* pages

- Lots of content can be customized and you can even create your own resources using the Create button

- You can navigate the resources by book and chapter, or use the simple search bar

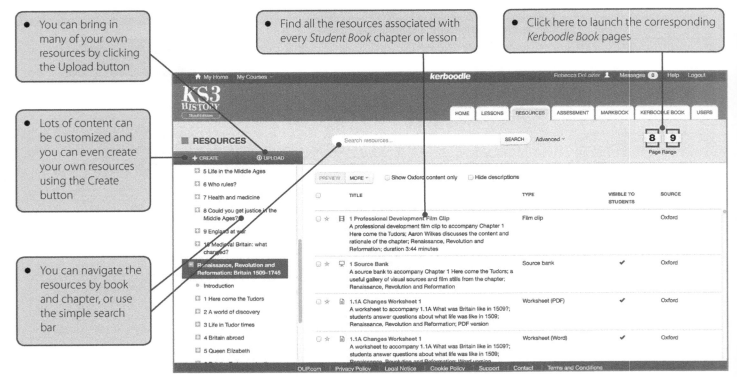

Renaissance, Revolution and Reformation: Britain 1509–1745 Kerboodle

The Resources section has more than:

 20 film clips: Specially-commissioned film clips produced at a stunning English Heritage location to bring History to life in your classroom.

5 mini-movies: Short animated clips that cover topics in a visually stimulating and easy to understand way.

 75 worksheets: Worksheets include creative worksheets that help provide differentiation/extension material for each lesson, and film worksheets to help students analyse the History Squad films and link ideas back to the *Student Book* lesson. Worksheets are provided as PDFs, which you can print off and photocopy, and as Word files, which you can customize to suit your students' needs.

 70 History skills activities: A range of interactive activities for use on your whiteboard are available for each lesson. They target a number of history skills, concepts and processes: historical enquiry, chronological understanding, cultural, ethnic and religious diversity, change and continuity, cause and consequence, significance, interpretation, and using evidence.

They can also be used for independent study.

 10 source banks: A source bank with captions for each chapter is provided so you can easily enlarge any photo or written source from the *Student Book* on screen and use it as a discussion starter, use them in your own worksheets, or give them to students to use in class or homework activities.

Teacher support resources

Aaron Wilkes' professional development film clip for each chapter offers ideas and teaching tips to make history memorable for all your students. In these short films, he explains his rationale behind his approach to the *Student Books* and includes suggestions for practical delivery and assessment of the new 2014 National Curriculum.

Kerboodle Resources are fully integrated with the *Student Book*:

All the resources and assessments are completely matched to the *Renaissance, Revolution and Reformation: Britain 1509–1745 Student Book*.

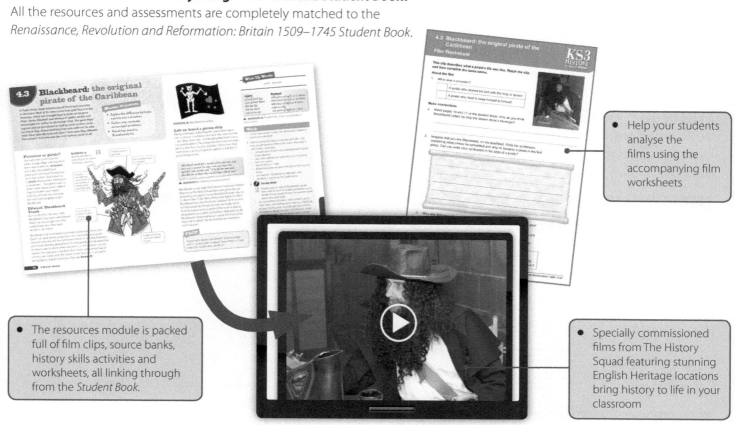

Help your students analyse the films using the accompanying film worksheets

The resources module is packed full of film clips, source banks, history skills activities and worksheets, all linking through from the *Student Book*.

Specially commissioned films from The History Squad featuring stunning English Heritage locations bring history to life in your classroom

Lessons

Click on the **Lessons tab** to access the full list of lesson presentations and plans for *Renaissance, Revolution and Reformation: Britain 1509–1745*.

Ready-to-play lesson presentations complement every lesson in the book. Each lesson presentation is easy to launch, and features unit objectives, the related starters, worksheets, film and interactive resources, and closes with a plenary activity. You can further personalize the lessons by adding in your own resources and notes. Your lessons and notes can be accessed by your whole department, and they are a great time-saver and **ideal for non-specialist** teachers and cover lessons.

The Lessons module contains ready-to-play lesson presentations and plans that complement every double-page spread in the book

- Every lesson is accompanied by teacher notes to fully support your lesson delivery

6.4 Lesson Presentation and Plan

'Fire burn and cauldron bubble'

Matthew Hopkins used sleep deprivation to extract confession from suspected witches, keeping them apart from their 'familiars' to weaken their alleged powers.

6.4 Dungeon Film Clip
You're about to watch a film in which two women discuss accusations of witchcraft.

6.4 Film Worksheet
What can we learn from this clip? This worksheet contains questions on what is covered in the film.

6.4 Dungeon Film Clip

6.4 Film Worksheet

Screen 4:
Main learning suggestions and assessment: What activities will take place? Students watch 6.4 Dungeon Film Clip in which two women discuss accusations of witchcraft. They then complete the activities in 6.4 Film Worksheet.

Screen 5:
Main learning suggestions and assessment: What activities will take place? Students can conduct a source analysis using 6.4 Using Evidence History Skills Activity.

Screen 6:
Another plenary suggestion for this lesson: Students could compare the popular image of witches and wizards and discuss whether the former is misogynistic by comparison.

LESSON NOTES | Tools | Digital Book | Back | 4 of 6 | Next

- Resources are built into each presentation so all the relevant activities, films and worksheets are ready to launch

The resources you want to use can also be rearranged and launched in sequence to suit your classroom needs

- For each lesson, a printable set of teacher notes are also available as a guide to support your lesson delivery, and provide further ideas or tips that only teachers can see.

Renaissance, Revolution and Reformation: Britain 1509–1745 Lesson Presentation and Plan

Assessment

Click on the **Assessment tab** to find a wide range of assessment materials to help you deliver a varied, motivating, and effective assessment programme.

- a markbook and a reporting function help keep everything you need in one place

Skills are assessed through step-by-step assessment tasks and support materials

Knowledge-checks are automatically marked to save you time

Renaissance, Revolution and Reformation: Britain 1509–1745 Kerboodle Assessment module

To cover every chapter, the Assessment section provides:

- 🔝 **11 auto-marked tests:** Each end-of-chapter auto-marked test is a knowledge-check. The marks are automatically reported in the **Markbook tab** to help save time setting questions and marking.

- 📄 **11 self-assessment worksheets:** Self- and peer-assessment, opportunities are provided via 'I can…' checklists for each chapter, which encourage students to consider how far they and their peers have understood the concepts and developed skills relevant to that chapter.

In addition, there are also bespoke materials to support the Assessing Your Learning tasks:

- 🖥 **3 assessment task presentations:** Each assessment task in the *Student Book*, which assesses history **skills**, has a front-of-class presentation for you to use to help guide students towards unpacking the task and understanding what it is asking of them. You can lead students through this step-by-step presentation and help them decide how to prepare to complete the task.

- 📄 **3 success criteria teacher grids:** A grid accompanies each assessment task in the *Student Book*, which helps teachers mark the tasks in relation to such skills as evaluation, analysis, and understanding.

- 📄 **3 sets of assessment worksheets:** These worksheets complement the assessment tasks in the *Student Book* and the assessment task presentations. They recap the task, provide a self-evaluation chart, and space for students to prepare their work.

A **Markbook** with reporting function completes the *Kerboodle* assessment package, so you can keep track of all your students' test results and assessment scores. This includes both the auto-marked tests and work that needs to be marked by you. It is also easy to import class registers and create user accounts for all your students.

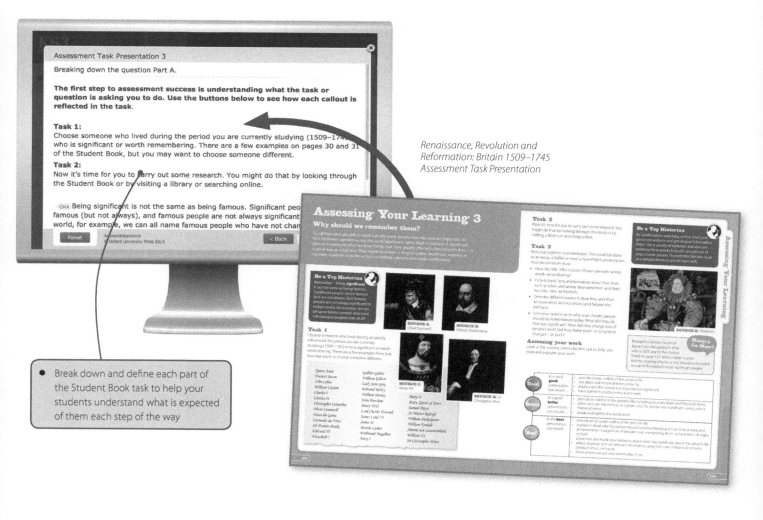

Renaissance, Revolution and Reformation: Britain 1509–1745 Assessment Task Presentation

- Break down and define each part of the Student Book task to help your students understand what is expected of them each step of the way

Assessment

Auto-marked tests

The *Renaissance, Revolution and Reformation Kerboodle* contains auto-marked tests for each chapter to help save you time setting questions and marking for historical knowledge and understanding. Each test contains between 10 and 15 questions and should take most students no more than half an hour. Test results are automatically stored in the markbook.

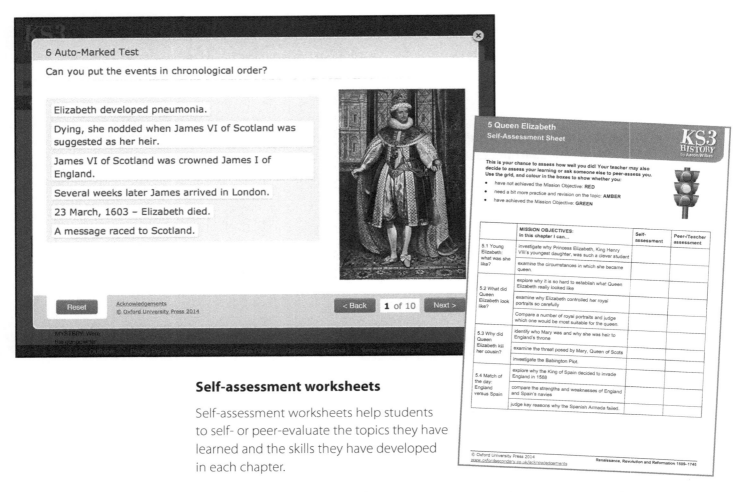

Self-assessment worksheets

Self-assessment worksheets help students to self- or peer-evaluate the topics they have learned and the skills they have developed in each chapter.

Digital markbook

A markbook and a reporting function complete the *Kerboodle* assessment package, so you can keep all your students' test results and assessment scores in one place. This can include the auto-marked tests as well as pieces of work you or the students have marked by hand.

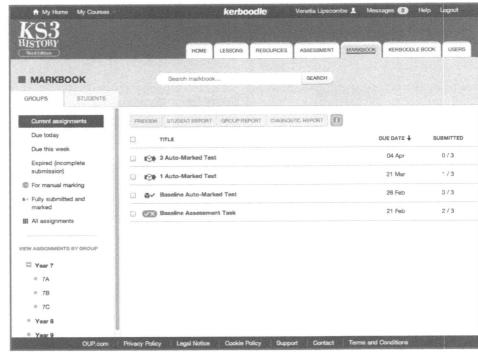

Assessing Your Learning tasks

On the *Renaissance, Revolution and Reformation Kerboodle*, you'll find resources to use when introducing the *Student Book* assessment tasks to the class. The success criteria teacher grids can help you mark the tasks in relation to such skills as evaluation, analysis, and understanding, whether you want to mark using National Curriculum levels, GCSE grade indicators, or performance levels.

You can use the *Assessing Your Learning assessment task presentations* to lead students step-by-step and help them decide how to complete the task.

Assessing Your Learning assessment worksheets accompany the tasks, so that once you finish the presentation your students can easily get started. They recap the task, include space for students to prepare their work, and provide a self-evaluation chart.

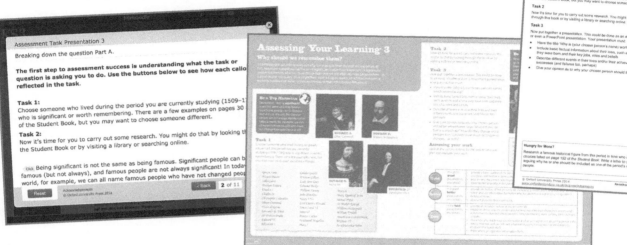

Kerboodle Book

The **Renaissance, Revolution and Reformation: Britain 1509–1745 Kerboodle Book** provides you with an on-screen version of the Student Book for you to use on your whiteboard with the whole class.

Teacher access to the *Kerboodle Book* is **automatically available** as part of the *Lessons, Resources and Assessment* package. You can also choose to buy access for your students.

Both teacher and student access include a simple **bank of tools** so you can **personalize** the book and take notes.

It can be accessed on other devices, such as tablets.

Every teacher and student has their own digital notebook for use within their *Kerboodle Book*. All user notes are accessible to themselves only

- You and your students can use different tools such as Sticky Notes, Bookmarks and Pencil features to personalize each page

- You can Zoom in and Spotlight any part of the text

- You can quickly navigate around the book with the contents menu, keyword search or page number search

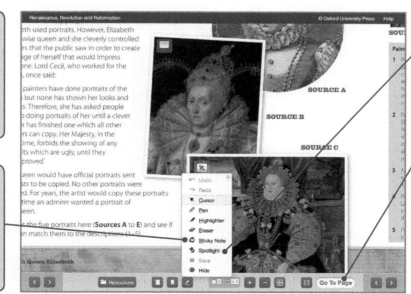

Overview:
Chapter 1 Here come the Tudors

Helping you deliver KS3 History National Curriculum

The Reformation (in both Europe and England), the Counter Reformation, and Elizabeth's religious settlement are covered in detail in this chapter. All three of these topics are given as examples of subject content which could be covered in the 2014 National Curriculum KS3 Programme of Study.

These topics contain very difficult concepts for young people to grasp. This chapter takes a straightforward, logical, and chronological route through this significant period in local, national, and international history. This should equip students well for the later chapters containing such equally difficult concepts as the Civil War, slavery, empire, and revolution.

The Big Picture

Why are we teaching 'Here come the Tudors'?

It was a straightforward decision to dedicate a whole chapter to the Tudor dynasty. First we paint a picture of what Britain was like in 1509, the year Henry VII died and his son became King Henry VIII. Setting the scene in this way should help students to grasp the enormity of the changes that take place as they work their way through the book. They will, of course, compare the Britain of 1509 with the Britain of 1745 towards the end of this book.

Students go on to examine the reigns of Henry VIII and his children, and their relationships with religion. Some of the more salacious and spectacular areas of their lives have also been included, but we have attempted to constantly refer back, or give prominence, to the religious aspects of their

Skills and processes covered in this chapter

		1.1A	1.1B	1.2	1.3	1.4	1.5	1.6	1.7	1.8	1.9	1.10
History skills	Historical enquiry	✓	✓					✓		✓		
	Using evidence and source work	✓		✓		✓		✓		✓	✓	
	Chronological understanding				✓	✓						
	Understanding cultural, ethnic and religious diversity	✓				✓	✓		✓	✓	✓	✓
	Change and continuity	✓	✓		✓				✓	✓		
	Cause and consequence			✓	✓	✓	✓	✓	✓	✓		✓
	Significance					✓			✓			
	Interpretations							✓		✓	✓	
	Making links/connections		✓								✓	
	Explores similarities and differences		✓		✓				✓			
Literacy and numeracy	Key words identified/deployed	✓	✓	✓	✓		✓	✓			✓	✓
	Extended writing				✓	✓		✓	✓			
	Encourages reading for meaning	✓	✓	✓	✓	✓	✓	✓	✓	✓	✓	✓
	Focuses on structuring writing					✓		✓				
	Asks students to use writing to explore and develop ideas				✓	✓		✓			✓	
	Learn through talk/discussion						✓				✓	
	Numeracy opportunities		✓							✓		
Activity types	Creative task			✓		✓			✓			
	Emphasizes role of individual			✓	✓		✓		✓	✓		✓
	Group work											
	Independent research		✓			✓			✓		✓	
	Develops study skills	✓	✓			✓		✓		✓		

reigns. This reinforces the influence of faith in the period. The chapter ends with the last Tudor monarch, Elizabeth, and focuses on her 'middle way'. This sets the students up nicely for a more detailed investigation of Queen Elizabeth later on in the book (chapter 5).

Lesson sequence

Lesson title	NC references	Objectives	Outcomes
1.1A What was Britain like in 1509? pp8–9 **1.1B What was Britain like in 1509? pp10–11**	Society, economy and culture across the period	• Examine what Britain was like in 1509. • Summarize England's relationship with its neighbouring countries. • Contrast Britain in 1509 with Britain today.	**All** students will be able to identify key features of life in Britain in 1509. **Most** students will be able to describe what life was like in 1509, using evidence to support their ideas. **Some** students will be able to make inferences from primary and secondary sources to describe what life was like in 1509.
1.2 What was young Henry VIII like? pp12–13	The English Reformation and Counter Reformation (Henry VIII to Mary I)	• Examine how young Henry VIII spent his time and money. • Judge how religious he was as a young man.	**All** students will be able to describe how Henry spent his time and money. **Most** students will be able to write for a specific audience and purpose. **Some** students will be able to analyse how 'Great' Henry VIII was.
1.3 Henry VIII, his first wife and his big problem pp14–15	The English Reformation and Counter Reformation (Henry VIII to Mary I)	• Explore how and why Henry VIII fell out with the Pope. • Examine how this affected the life of Henry and religion in the whole of England.	**All** students will identify different reasons why Henry VIII wanted to divorce Catherine of Aragon. **Most** students will explain at least one of these reasons. **Some** students will prioritize the reasons why Henry VIII wanted a divorce.
1.4 Who'd want to marry King Henry VIII? pp16–17	The English Reformation and Counter Reformation (Henry VIII to Mary I)	• Explain why Henry married so many women. • Examine what happened to each of his wives. • Advise his sixth wife on how to survive being married to Henry.	**All** students will describe why Henry married each of his wives and what problems there were in their marriages. **Most** students will use the information about Henry's marriages to make inferences regarding what Katherine Parr could do to keep on his good side! **Some** students will use evidence to work out and explain which of Henry's wives was his favourite.
1.5 What did Protestants protest about? pp18–19	The English Reformation and Counter Reformation (Henry VIII to Mary I)	• Explain why some people criticized the Catholic Church. • Examine how Protestants got their name and what they believed.	**All** students will match causes to their consequences. **Most** students will create their own 'cause' cards to match to consequences. **Some** students will create both 'cause' and 'consequence' cards.
1.6 History Mystery: Why did the *Mary Rose* sink? pp20–21		• Examine a variety of evidence relating to Henry VIII's favourite ship. • Propose how the *Mary Rose* sank.	**All** students will categorize sources by deciding which theory they support. **Most** students will decide which theory they think is most likely and why. **Some** students will analyse sources to decide how reliable they are, and then use this information to decide why the *Mary Rose* sank.
1.7 Edward VI: the boy king pp22–23	The English Reformation and Counter Reformation (Henry VIII to Mary I)	• Explain how and why Henry's son changed religion in England. • Decide what kind of boy Edward VI was.	**All** students will identify how religion changed under Edward VI. **Most** students will describe how religion changed under Edward VI. **Some** students will explain why these changes occurred.
1.8 How bloody was Bloody Mary? pp24–25	The English Reformation and Counter Reformation (Henry VIII to Mary I)	• Examine how and why Bloody Mary got her nickname. • Decide whether she deserved her nasty nickname.	**All** students will identify evidence to be used for and against Mary. **Most** students will use evidence to explain one interpretation of Mary. **Some** students will analyse the different interpretations of Mary, deciding which they think is most accurate.
1.9 The nastiest nursery rhyme in the world! pp26–27	The English Reformation and Counter Reformation (Henry VIII to Mary I)	• Examine the hidden meaning of the popular nursery rhyme 'Mary, Mary, quite contrary'. • Decide which religion the writer of the rhyme would have belonged to.	**All** students will explain what each line of the nursery rhyme means. **Most** students will explain why this interpretation of Mary exists. **Some** students will use evidence to provide an alternative interpretation of Mary.
1.10 Elizabeth's middle way pp28–29	The Elizabethan religious settlement and conflict with Catholics (including Scotland, Spain and Ireland)	• Analyse how Elizabeth tried to end religious turmoil in Tudor England. • Recall which faith Elizabeth belonged to. • Explain how this caused another Catholic clampdown.	**All** students will identify how the Pope reacted to Elizabeth's middle way. **Most** students will describe the Pope's reaction to the religious changes that Elizabeth made, and the way she reacted to his declarations. **Some** students will analyse how successful Elizabeth's middle way was.
Assessing Your Learning 1 pp30–33	The English Reformation and Counter Reformation (Henry VIII to Mary I)	• Examine the reigns of Henry VIII, Edward VI, Mary I and Elizabeth I and judge who was the 'best' monarch against a set of criteria.	**All** students will describe each monarch and explain something they each did. **Most** students will assess both the successful and unsuccessful actions of each monarch. **Some** students will explain and justify who they have chosen as the 'best' monarch in relation to the other monarchs.

Ideas for enrichment

You could set students a research task on some very tough concepts, for example:

- The Ninety-Five Theses
- Act of Supremacy 1534
- Book of Common Prayer.

Refer students back to the famous nursery rhyme 'Mary, Mary, quite contrary'. You could ask them to research the origins of others, such as 'Humpty Dumpty' or 'Baa, Baa, Black Sheep'. Obviously, an excellent school trip destination could be the Mary Rose Museum at Historic Dockyards in Portsmouth.

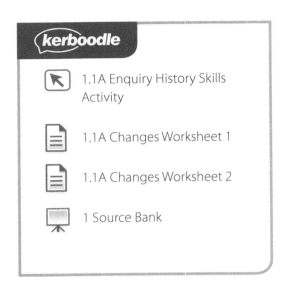

Renaissance, Revolution and Reformation pages 8–9

Lesson summary

Students will create a 'Beginner's Guide to Ruling Britain' in which they summarize what it was like to live in Britain in 1509.

What are the lesson outcomes?

All students will be able to identify key features of life in Britain in 1509.

Most students will be able to describe what life was like in 1509, using evidence to support their ideas.

Some students will be able to make inferences from primary and secondary sources to describe what life was like in 1509.

Starter suggestion

- Show students the contents of a mystery person's dustbin and ask them to make inferences about what kind of person they might be. For example, a bus pass might lead students to infer that the person does not drive; or a discarded lipstick that the person is female.

Main learning suggestions and assessment

What activities will take place?

Task 1: Students should read the information on pages 8–9 and then use it to create a 'Beginner's Guide to Ruling Britain' for Henry VIII in 1509. Students will need to decide which categories to sort the information into, such as 'Who you can trust' or 'Problems you might face'. Then they need to decide which details to include in each category.

Task 2: Students should complete Work activities **1** and **2** on page 9.

Task 3: Students could complete a mind-map summarizing what Britain was like in 1509. Changes Worksheet 2 provides

a framework for this. Students could also consolidate their knowledge of life in 1509 using Changes Worksheet 1.

How will students demonstrate their understanding?

Creating a 'Beginner's Guide to Ruling Britain' will introduce students to the idea of selecting evidence from secondary sources and making inferences from it.

Plenary suggestions

- Students can complete 1.1A Enquiry History Skills Activity, either individually on laptops or tablets, or as a class with the test displayed on an electronic whiteboard. In this activity students use information about Britain in 1509 to develop enquiry skills.

Differentiation suggestions

Support

- A basic writing frame or list of categories to consider could be provided to support lower ability students. For example, they could use categories such as: Enemies; Friends; Religion; Education.

- In Work activity **2**, students must draw a bar chart. It might be helpful for you to model this on the board so students are clear about what is expected of them.

Extension: Hungry for more?

- Students could research one or more of the categories mentioned in **Source B** on page 9, and use the information to create a 'What's hot and what's not' article for a magazine from 1509. They should draw a large thermometer in the middle of the page and position the information they have researched alongside the thermometer, according to its popularity at the time. They should write a line for each factor and possibly add an illustration.

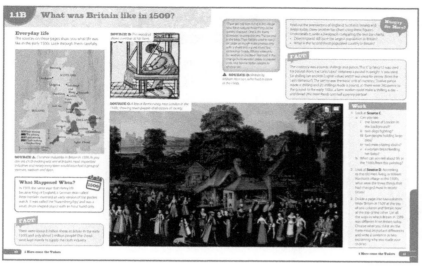

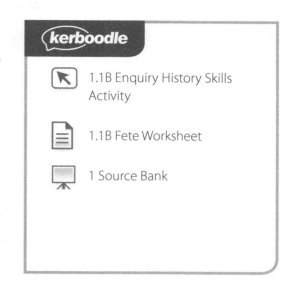

Renaissance, Revolution and Reformation pages 10–11

Lesson summary

Students will use and select evidence from primary sources to support historical inferences. This lesson includes a focus on literacy skills.

What are the lesson outcomes?

All students will be able to identify key features of life in Britain in 1509.

Most students will be able to describe what life was like in 1509, using evidence to support their ideas.

Some students will be able to make inferences from primary and secondary sources to describe what life was like in 1509.

Point	Source	Evidence
Textiles were the biggest industry in Britain.		
Most settlements had fewer than 6000 people living in them.		
Punishments were similar to those used in the medieval era.		
Some people were getting richer.		

Starter suggestion

- Students should consolidate their knowledge from lesson 1.1A by writing down a list of three words that describe what life was like in 1509. They should then choose their favourite word and explain to the rest of the class why they chose this one.

Main learning suggestions and assessment

What activities will take place?

Task 1: Students should read through the sources on pages 10–11 and then create an evidence table, as follows, using the sources to prove statements. Students should first identify which sources they are using, and then they should either select a quotation from a written source or describe part of a visual source for their evidence.

Task 2: Students should complete Work activities **1–3** on page 11. They should use evidence and inferences from the sources to consolidate the skills they have developed in **Task 1**. 1.1B Fete Worksheet supports Work activity **1**.

How will students demonstrate their understanding?

Task 1 will allow students to demonstrate their ability to select and use evidence from sources to support an inference.

Plenary suggestions

- Students could create a 'spot the difference' game by drawing a modern version of **Source C**, showing activities that might happen at a school, village or church fete today. How is life different?

Differentiation suggestions

Support

- Students could be directed towards sensible sources in the *Student Book* to use for evidence in **Task 1**.

Extension: Hungry for more?

- Students could be given the sources to use in **Task 1**, but asked to create their own 'points' in the evidence table.

1.2 What was young Henry VIII like?

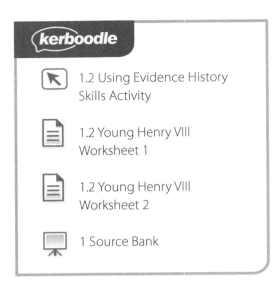

Renaissance, Revolution and Reformation pages 12–13

Lesson summary

Students will create an online dating profile for Henry VIII, describing what kind of man he was, before making a judgment on whether or not he was 'Great'. This lesson includes a focus on literacy (different writing styles).

What are the lesson outcomes?

All students will be able to describe how Henry spent his time and money.

Most students will be able to write for a specific audience and purpose.

Some students will be able to analyse how 'Great' Henry VIII was.

Starter suggestion

● Students should draw and label an image of Henry VIII, based on their preconceptions of him.

Main learning suggestions and assessment

What activities will take place?

Task 1: Henry VIII has earned a reputation as a bit of a womaniser! Students should read the information on pages 12–13 and then create a profile for him to appear on an online dating site called 'Matchmakers for Monarchs'. In the profile they should describe how Henry VIII spent his time and his money. A variation of this activity is available in 1.2 Young Henry VIII Worksheet 1.

Task 2: In pairs or small groups, students should write a list of words to describe the kind of women they think Henry would be interested in dating (and marrying!). They should then sort these words in order of importance.

Task 3: Students should write a paragraph explaining whether or not they feel Henry VIII deserved the title 'Henry the Great', and then complete Worksheet 2, which will help consolidate their knowledge of young Henry VIII.

How will students demonstrate their understanding?

In **Task 1** students will demonstrate their ability to select and use evidence and write in an informal manner. In **Task 3** students will demonstrate their ability to analyse an interpretation of Henry VIII.

Plenary suggestions

● One student should be Henry VIII and the others should write a single word on a mini-whiteboard to describe the kind of woman they think he should date. Each 'contestant' should stand up and 'Henry' can ask them to sit down if he is not interested in their description. At the end, 'Henry' must explain why he has chosen his 'date', using evidence from the lesson in his explanation.

Differentiation suggestions

Support

● Lower ability students could be given a template to complete for Henry's profile, which includes question prompts to scaffold their answers.

Extension: Hungry for more?

● Students could write two paragraphs in **Task 3**, explaining both sides of the argument by finding evidence of Henry VIII's 'greatness' and weaknesses.

● Students could complete 1.2 Using Evidence History Skills Activity to further investigate the historical interpretations of Henry VIII and develop skills relating to the analysis of sources.

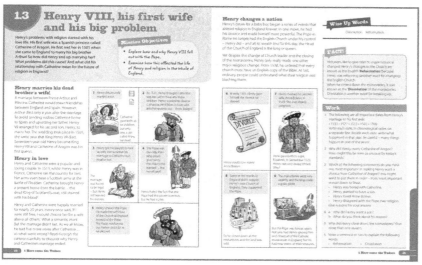

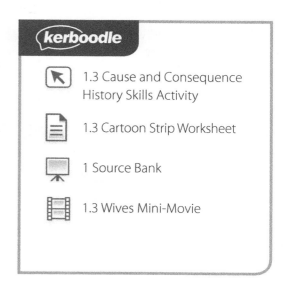

Renaissance, Revolution and Reformation pages 14–15

Lesson summary

Students will create a piece of extended writing, in the form of a letter to the Pope, explaining why Henry VIII wants a divorce. This lesson includes a focus on literacy.

What are the lesson outcomes?

All students will identify different reasons why Henry VIII wanted to divorce Catherine of Aragon.

Most students will explain at least one of these reasons.

Some students will prioritize the reasons why Henry VIII wanted a divorce.

Starter suggestion

- Students could consolidate their knowledge of Henry VIII from the previous lesson by creating a spider diagram to describe what kind of king Henry was.

Main learning suggestions and assessment

What activities will take place?

Task 1: Students should read the information on pages 14–15 and/or watch 1.3 Wives Mini-Movie. This narrated animation explains why Henry wanted to break away from Rome and how he went about doing so. Students should then write a letter from Henry VIII to the Pope, asking for a divorce from Catherine and explaining why he wants this.

Task 2: Students should pretend that Henry VIII has received a reply from the Pope, stating his refusal to allow a divorce from Catherine. They should write a second letter from Henry to a friend, explaining how he plans to settle the issue and how this will benefit him personally and financially.

Task 3: Students should complete Work activities **1–6** on page 15. 1.3 Cartoon Strip Worksheet helps support activity **1**.

Students should further their understanding of cause and consequence by completing the History skills activity for this lesson. In this task, students prioritise causes.

How will students demonstrate their understanding?

The extended writing activities in **Tasks 1** and **2** will develop students' abilities to explain cause and consequence. The work produced can be used as formative assessment to test whether students are able to identify, describe, explain, evaluate, and analyse factors.

Plenary suggestions

- In small groups, students could be given cards with the four reasons for Henry VIII's divorce, as identified in Work activity **3**. They could be asked to put them in order of how important each reason was, and then explain their ideas to the rest of the group.

Differentiation suggestions

Support

- Writing frames could be produced for lower ability students, helping them to scaffold their letters.

Extension: Hungry for more?

- For homework, students could produce an essay entitled 'Why did Henry VIII want to divorce Catherine of Aragon?' in which they explain the four reasons identified in the plenary. They should write a conclusion where they analyse which was the most important reason.

1.4 Who'd want to marry King Henry VIII?

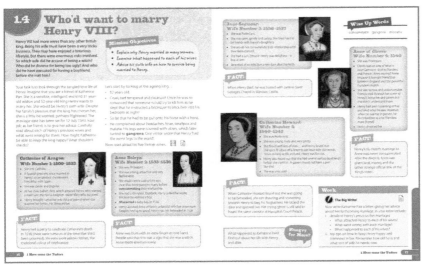

Renaissance, Revolution and Reformation pages 16–17

Lesson summary

Students will create an 'Agony Aunt' magazine article advising Katherine Parr about where Henry VIII's previous wives went wrong and how to keep him happy.

What are the lesson outcomes?

All students will describe why Henry married each of his wives and what problems there were in their marriages.

Most students will use the information about Henry's marriages to make inferences regarding what Katherine Parr could do to keep on his good side!

Some students will use evidence to work out and explain which of Henry's wives was his favourite.

Starter suggestion

- Ask students to create a mini-timeline to put the wives of Henry VIII in chronological order.

Main learning suggestions and assessment

What activities will take place?

Task 1: Students should read the information on pages 16–17 and then either complete the Work activities or a variation in which they create an 'Agony Aunt' article for a magazine. In the article, students should include a letter from Katherine Parr to the Agony Aunt, asking for advice about her forthcoming marriage.

Task 2: Students should watch 1.4 Katherine Film Clip and complete the accompanying worksheet. They could also complete 1.4 Significance History Skills Activity.

How will students demonstrate their understanding?

Completing **Task 1** (or a differentiated version of it) will enable students to develop their skills of summarizing evidence and making inferences from it by using the information to advise Katherine Parr about the kind of woman Henry is after.

Plenary suggestions

- Students could be asked to prepare a 'hot seat' activity. Split the class into six groups. Each should prepare one role, choosing between Henry VIII and the five wives that they have learned about in detail (leaving Katherine Parr out). Each group should elect one spokesperson. 'Henry' should take the hot seat first, explaining what he is looking for in a wife. This will consolidate students' knowledge from previous lessons. Then, each 'wife' will sum up her experiences. Each group should then order each of the 'wives' according to which they think was Henry's favourite. They should explain their ideas to the rest of the class.

Differentiation suggestions

Support

- Rather than completing a letter or magazine article, lower ability students could be asked to create a fact file or summary table for Henry's wives: For each wife, they should state: name; date of marriage; why Henry married her; marriage problems; how the marriage ended.

- 1.4 Advice Worksheet provides success criteria for the letter to Katherine. Otherwise, remind students of the conventions of a letter, such as including the date and addresses.

Extension: Hungry for more?

- Students could complete the 'Hungry for More' activity on page 17. They could use their research to complete an exclusive magazine interview with Henry VIII and his new wife.

1.5 What did Protestants protest about?

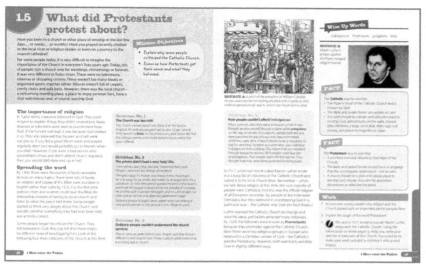

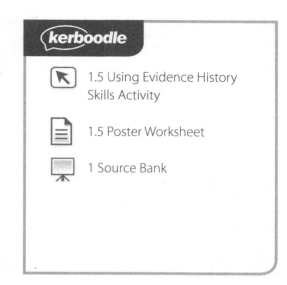

Renaissance, Revolution and Reformation pages 18–19

Lesson summary

Students will learn about cause and consequence by doing a 'matching pairs' activity.

What are the lesson outcomes?

All students will match causes to their consequences.

Most students will create their own 'cause' cards to match to consequences.

Some students will create both 'cause' and 'consequence' cards.

Starter suggestion

- Students could be introduced to the concept of cause and consequence, whilst consolidating previous learning, by being asking to match ideas together, such as:
Cause: Henry wanted a good relationship with Spain.
Consequence: Henry married Catherine of Aragon.

Main learning suggestions and assessment

What activities will take place?

Task 1: Students should read pages 18–19 and use the information to create 'cause' and 'consequence' cards. They should use these in a game of 'matching pairs'. Ideas for matching pairs are as follows:

Cause:
The printing press was invented.
People had to give 10% of their harvest to the Church.
The Bible was written in Latin, and church services were also in this language.

Consequence:
Books allowed people to share ideas and encouraged people to question religious ideas.
Poor people resented the Church, especially rich bishops.
People found it hard to feel close to God, as they didn't understand Latin.

Task 2: Students can play either 'matching pairs' or 'snap' with the cards they have created.

Task 3: Students should complete 1.5 Using Evidence History Skills Activity.

How will students demonstrate their understanding?

By matching or creating cause and consequence pairs, students will demonstrate their understanding of how and why Luther challenged the Catholic Church as well as their ability to link cause and consequence.

Plenary suggestions

- Students could be given a 'cause' or 'consequence' card. They should then move around the classroom until they find their partner, and stand next to them.

Differentiation suggestions

Support

- Lower ability students could be given pre-prepared 'cause' and 'consequence' cards to sort and then match.

Extension: Hungry for more?

- Students could complete 1.5 Poster Worksheet. This includes an extension task that encourages students to question the significance of the printing press in spreading religious ideas.

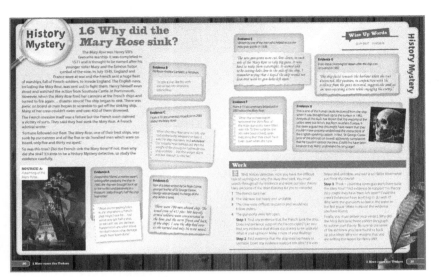

Renaissance, Revolution and Reformation pages 20–21

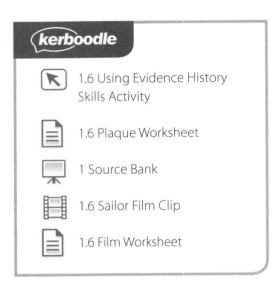

Lesson summary

Students will solve the History Mystery of why the *Mary Rose* sank, first by matching evidence to the different theories and then by working out how reliable this evidence is.

What are the lesson outcomes?

All students will categorize sources by deciding which theory they support.

Most students will decide which theory they think is most likely and why.

Some students will analyse sources to decide how reliable they are, and then use this information to decide why the *Mary Rose* sank.

Starter suggestion

- Students could be shown an image of the *Mary Rose* (such as **Source A**) and be asked to think of three words that describe the ship.

Main learning suggestions and assessment

What activities will take place?

Task 1: Students should read through the information on pages 20–21 and then complete the Work activities. They need to find evidence to support the different theories about why the *Mary Rose* sank.

Task 2: Students should focus their investigation on **Sources E**, **F** and **H** and work out how reliable they are. They should ask: What is it?; Who created the source?; Where was it created?; When was it created?; Why was it created? These can either be discussed in small groups or written out as questions and answers for each source.

Task 3: Students should add a second paragraph to the conclusion they wrote as part of **Task 1**. Have they changed their minds since considering the reliability of the sources?

Task 4: Students should watch 1.6 Sailor Film Clip. They should then complete either 1.6 Film Worksheet or 1.6 Plaque Worksheet.

How will students demonstrate their understanding?

Students will write two paragraphs, one explaining which theory they think is most likely and why, and the other considering how the reliability of sources might hinder a historical enquiry.

Plenary suggestions

- Students could come up with success criteria for their written work through a group discussion. They then swap and peer-assess each other's written work, by writing down one thing that was done well and one thing they could improve. Students should then reclaim their work and be given an opportunity to improve it according to the target they have been set.

Differentiation suggestions

Support

- For **Task 1** kinaesthetic learners could be given the different sources as cards to sort into groups, according to which theory they support. The History skills activity for this lesson also helps students to analyse the evidence.

Extension: Hungry for more?

- Students could complete an essay entitled 'Why did the *Mary Rose* sink?' in which they explain the evidence supporting each of the four theories before analysing the evidence to reach a final conclusion. This activity could be used as formative assessment, to help set targets and support students in developing History skills.

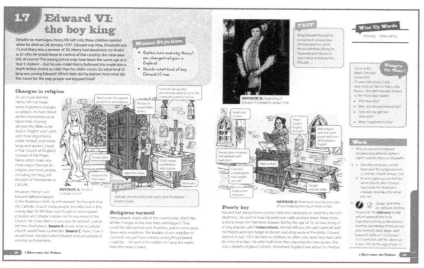

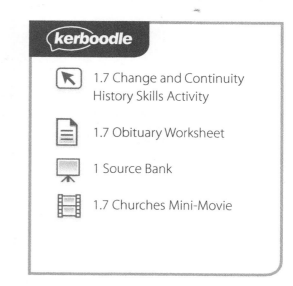

Renaissance, Revolution and Reformation pages 22–23

Lesson summary

Students will complete a series of tasks and activities to demonstrate their understanding of how religion changed under Edward VI.

What are the lesson outcomes?

All students will identify how religion changed under Edward VI.

Most students will describe how religion changed under Edward VI.

Some students will explain why these changes occurred.

Starter suggestion

- Students could be given a list of features of churches. They need to sort each feature into whether it would be found in a Catholic church or a Protestant church. This consolidates knowledge from *1.5 What did Protestants protest about?*

Main learning suggestions and assessment

What activities will take place?

Task 1: Students should complete Work activities **1–3** on page 23.

Task 2: Students should write a sermon to be given in a Protestant church, explaining why the Protestant way of worshipping is 'better' than the Catholic way. This could include details about how Edward VI will punish anyone who does not follow his preferred method of worship!

Task 3: Students should complete the History skills activity for this lesson, in which they consider change and continuity in churches during the reign of Edward VI.

How will students demonstrate their understanding?

The written activities in this lesson will enable students to demonstrate whether they are able to identify, describe and explain ideas.

Plenary suggestions

- The class could play 'taboo word'. One student sits with their back to an interactive whiteboard. A key word appears on the screen, along with a list of related words. The rest of the class need to give clues to describe and explain the key word, without using any of the other words listed. The student needs to guess what the key word is.

Differentiation suggestions

Support

- Rather than describing the different types of churches in Work activity **2**, lower ability students could create their own 'spot the difference' game based on the two types of churches.

- Students could complete 1.7 Obituary Worksheet instead of Work activity **3**. Otherwise, you might like to model an obituary and explain that they sometimes start with the most important event in someone's life, rather than being in chronological order.

Extension: Hungry for more?

- Students could research Lady Jane Grey. They could use the information they find to create either a leaflet or a poster, campaigning for her to be made queen after Edward VI.

- Students could find out what happened to the trees leading up to Jane's house when she was executed.

1.8 How bloody was Bloody Mary?

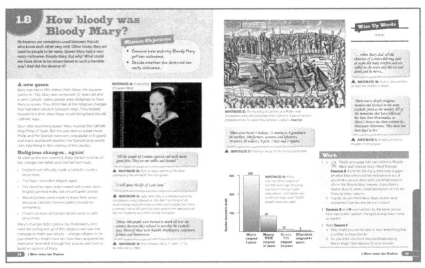

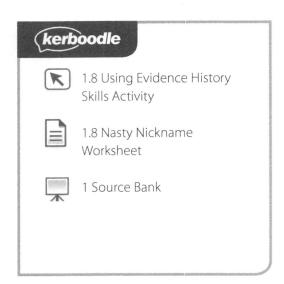

Renaissance, Revolution and Reformation pages 24–25

Lesson summary

Students will analyse different historical interpretations of Mary Tudor to decide whether she was 'bloody' or just 'misunderstood'.

What are the lesson outcomes?

All students will identify evidence to be used for and against Mary.

Most students will use evidence to explain one interpretation of Mary.

Some students will analyse the different interpretations of Mary, deciding which they think is most accurate.

Starter suggestion

- Students could be given a list of historical nicknames and asked if they can work out who they refer to. For example, the Virgin Queen, Bloody Mary, or Softsword. The nicknames chosen could depend on where your school is and what your students have previously studied.

Main learning suggestions and assessment

What activities will take place?

Task 1: Students should read through the information on pages 24–25. They should draw around each of their hands, then label one palm 'Bloody Mary' and the other 'Misunderstood Mary'. On the finger of each hand they should write one fact or piece of evidence from a source that supports the viewpoint. Students should be warned that they may not be able to fill both hands.

Task 2: Students should complete 1.8 Using Evidence History Skills Activity, focusing on how Mary has been interpreted and why. Students could complete Work activities **1–3** on page 25.

How will students demonstrate their understanding?

Students will select and summarize evidence on their 'hands' and could then be asked to turn this into an essay for homework. They should use the expression 'on one hand… on the other hand' in this activity, to help them see that there are often two sides to an argument in history.

Plenary suggestions

- Students could play a game called 'splat'. Key words are written on a board (or on an A3 sheet of paper stuck to the wall) and two students stand, one on each side of the key words, with rulers. Another member of the class gives a clue and the contestants have to 'splat' the correct answer with their ruler. Whoever gets the correct answer first stays up for the next round and whoever posed the clue becomes the next contestant.

Differentiation suggestions

Support

- For **Task 1** lower ability students could be given strips of paper with different evidence. They use these to stick onto the fingers of the correct hand. 1.8 Nasty Nickname Worksheet provides an alternative framework for this activity.

- For **Task 2** peer support could be used, with students of different abilities being teamed together to complete the activity.

Extension: Hungry for more?

- Mary may have been the victim of biased historians depicting her as an evil and bloodthirsty queen. Ask students if they can find any historians who are more favourable towards Mary. What do they say about her?

1.9 The nastiest nursery rhyme in the world!

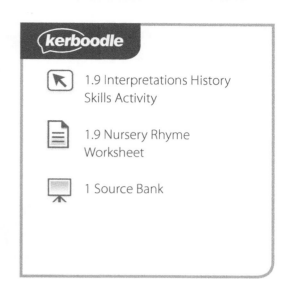

Renaissance, Revolution and Reformation pages 26–27

Lesson summary

Students will use logic and reasoning to work out the meaning of a nursery rhyme and then use their prior knowledge to put it into its historical context.

What are the lesson outcomes?

All students will explain what each line of the nursery rhyme, 'Mary, Mary, quite contrary', means.

Most students will explain why this interpretation of Mary exists.

Some students will use evidence to provide an alternative interpretation of Mary.

Starter suggestion

- Students could be given a copy of the nursery rhyme, 'Mary, Mary, quite contrary', and asked to illustrate it for a children's book. They could also describe what kind of images they chose and why.

Main learning suggestions and assessment

What activities will take place?

Task 1: Students should complete Work activities **1–4** on page 27.

Task 2: Students should imagine for this activity that they are working in Mary's Ministry of Propaganda. They have been tasked with writing a new nursery rhyme about her, this time standing up for her.

Task 3: Students should complete 1.9 Interpretations History Skills Activity, which focuses in detail on the lines of the nursery rhyme.

Task 4: Students should examine **Source A** in the *Student Book*, or in the source bank for this chapter, and analyse how useful it is for a historian by considering what it tells us about Mary and by explaining its limitations.

How will students demonstrate their understanding?

Students explain the historical significance of each of the lines of the nursery rhyme, demonstrating their abilities to use creative reasoning. They then use their prior knowledge of the era to put the nursery rhyme in context. In **Task 2** students use their prior knowledge to present an alternative interpretation of Mary.

Plenary suggestions

- Students could share the nursery rhymes that they have created in **Task 2**. The rest of the class could try to put each line into its historical context by suggesting what it is referencing.

Differentiation suggestions

Support

- To allow lower ability students to concentrate on acquiring new skills, rather than the logistics of copying out the nursery rhyme, they could complete 1.9 Nursery Rhyme Worksheet instead of Work activity **1**.

- Where more appropriate for **Task 2**, students could write a diary entry for Mary explaining how she feels about the nursery rhyme and why she feels that it is unfair.

- For Work activity **4**, you might want to give students an opening line, such as, 'I know the rhyme sounds nasty, but Mary did lots of horrid things when she was queen, so she asked for it! For example…'

Extension: Hungry for more?

- Students could complete the 'Hungry for More' activity on page 27 by researching the true meaning of other nursery rhymes.

Renaissance, Revolution and Reformation pages 28–29

Lesson summary

Students consider short-term, medium-term, and long-term effects, by studying the legacy of Elizabeth's middle way.

What are the lesson outcomes?

All students will identify how the Pope reacted to Elizabeth's middle way.

Most students will describe the Pope's reaction to the religious changes that Elizabeth made, and the way she reacted to his declarations.

Some students will analyse how successful Elizabeth's middle way was.

Starter suggestion

- Students could read the introduction text on page 28 and make a list of the problems Elizabeth would have faced when she became queen.

Main learning suggestions and assessment

What activities will take place?

Task 1: Students should read through the information on pages 28–29 and then write three answers for Work activity **3b**: a 'short-term' answer, a 'medium-term' answer, and a 'long-term' answer. The 'short-term' answer should be an opinion about whether Elizabeth's compromises would please everyone. The 'medium-term' answer should be about the Pope's reaction and what Elizabeth changed because of this. The 'long-term' answer should be about Elizabeth's religious legacy today. How have her actions affected our lives today?

Task 2: Students should pretend that they work for the Pope and create a 'wanted' poster for Elizabeth.

The poster should include details about what Elizabeth did that Catholics were not happy about, and what reward the Pope is offering.

Task 3: Students should complete 1.10 Understanding Diversity History Skills Activity, in which they explain the diverse experiences of different religious groups during Elizabeth's reign.

How will students demonstrate their understanding?

Students develop understanding of short-term, medium-term, and long-term consequences. They summarize ideas about how successful Elizabeth was by creating the poster in **Task 2**.

Plenary suggestions

- You could display statements on an interactive whiteboard, which describe a measure taken by Elizabeth. Students can demonstrate their knowledge of the topic by moving to different parts of the room to show whether Elizabeth's actions were designed to please Catholics or Protestants.

- Students could complete 1.10 Compromise Worksheet to consolidate their knowledge.

Differentiation suggestions

Support

- In **Task 1**, lower ability students could be given three sentences explaining the short-term, medium-term, and long-term consequences of Elizabeth's actions. They could label these appropriately, rather than writing their own explanations.

Extension: Hungry for more?

- Students could write a letter to the Pope from a priest in hiding in England, explaining what changes Elizabeth has made following the Pope's declarations against her. How has life become harder for Catholics in Elizabethan England?

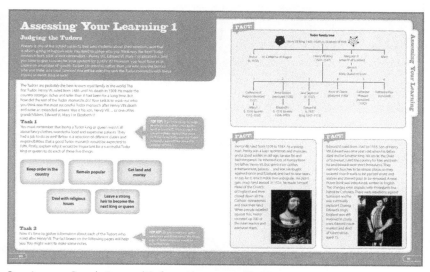

Renaissance, Revolution and Reformation pages 30–31

Student Book
- Assessment task
- Student 'Assessing your work' grid

kerboodle

Assessment Task Presentation 1

Assessment Worksheet 1

Success Criteria Teacher Grid 1

Teacher Handbook
- Success Criteria Teacher Grid 1

Assessment in the *Student Book*

In this assessment task, students are asked to complete a piece of extended writing to judge each of the Tudor monarchs against five criteria in order to analyse which was the most successful. The development of Church, state and society in Britain 1509–1745 is one of the areas that students should be taught at Key Stage 3, according to the 2014 History National Curriculum. The English Reformation, Counter-Reformation, and Elizabethan religious settlement and conflict are non-statutory examples of how this can be fulfilled.

In the *Student Book* (and on the supporting worksheets) you will find guidance on success criteria that you can use to help your students understand what their work should include. You could ask them to use these criteria for self- or peer-assessment once they have completed the task.

Chapter 1 Here come the Tudors assessment task

Your task is to work out who you think was the most successful Tudor monarch after Henry VII's death, and write an extended answer. Was it his son, Henry VIII… or one of his grandchildren, Edward VI, Mary I or Elizabeth I?

Make sure you:
- write about each of the monarchs featured in this assessment
- say what each monarch did well… and what they did badly
- explain your criteria for judging them
- conclude your answer with who you think was the most successful and why. Why have you awarded the stars you have given to each one?

Hungry for More?

Where does the first Tudor monarch (Henry VII) fit in? Find out about Henry VIII's father (and Mary, Elizabeth and Edward's grandfather) and work out where he'd fit in on your Tudor line-up. Judge him using the same criteria that you've judged the other four with. Would he be the most successful… or not?

Assessing your work

In a **good** extended answer, you would…	• describe each monarch • say what each monarch achieved (or didn't achieve) • use dates and historical terms correctly • have a basic structure.
In a **better** extended answer, you would…	• describe each monarch in detail • select and use information to explain what each monarch did successfully (or not so successfully) • use the correct dates and proper historical terms • produce well-structured work and include a conclusion about which monarch you think was the most successful.
In the **best** extended answer, you would…	• explain how you decided to judge the monarchs • show why you think some Tudor monarchs were more successful than others • select, organize and use relevant information and the correct historical terms to produce structured work • include a conclusion that sums up your findings.

Differentiation

- The best work will be structured like an essay and include a conclusion.

- You can support lower ability students by: 1) using the planning chart on page 32 of the *Student Book;* 2) giving advice on how to structure their answer; and 3) creating a writing frame for the essay based on the assessment criteria.

Success criteria teacher grid

Assessment criteria	Beginning/ Developing	Securing	Extending
	Current NC Level 3/4	Current NC Level 5/6	Current NC Level 7/8
	GCSE Grade Indicator E/D	GCSE Grade Indicator C/B	GCSE Grade Indicator A/A*
Remembering	Student can recall three facts about each monarch	Student can recall at least three actions or decisions that each monarch took	
Understanding	Student can explain what is meant by a success and what is meant by a failure	Student can describe some successes and failures of each monarch	Student can explain why some actions made each monarch successful and others were considered failures
Applying	Student can classify some actions of each monarch into successes and failures	Student begins to compare successes and failures of each monarch under the headings provided	Student can successfully compare and contrast each monarch's successes and failures under the criteria provided
Analyzing	Student can provide each monarch with a star rating for each heading	Student can explain their rating with a historical example	Student can use these ratings to compare each monarch and make a judgement on their overall success
Evaluating	Student can identify who they think the most successful monarch was	Student can justify their choice of most successful monarch with examples	Student can rank each monarch based on the criteria provided and explain why they have put them in the order they have chosen
Creating	Student attempts to use the correct historical terminology and their answer is structured appropriately	Student's answer is well structured and includes a conclusion about which monarch they thought was the most successful	Student selects, organizes and uses relevant information, including the correct historical terms, to produce a well-structured piece of work with a conclusion

Helping you deliver KS3 History National Curriculum

The 'golden age' of exploration is a must-do topic for any teacher covering the years 1509–1745. So too is the Renaissance. These two topics are defined and introduced in this chapter. They help to set up a more detailed examination of the growth of Britain's empire in America and India, and the key developments in science and technology, later in the book.

Students will have opportunities to explore several key concepts and develop their History skills. They need to think for themselves, use sources, be creative, think about significance, and place the history of Britain within the context of the wider world. Indeed, ensuring that students know and understand how Britain has influenced and has been influenced by the wider world is one of the key aims of the KS3 National Curriculum for History!

The Big Picture

Why are we teaching 'A world of discovery'?

Featuring Martellus' famous 1489 map of the world, students begin this chapter with the idea of the 'known world' from a European perspective. They then move on to examine the attraction of foreign lands to European explorers (and monarchs), and they consider how advances in shipping and navigation helped to contribute to the accidental discovery of a 'new world' in the 1490s. This leads neatly onto the exploits of da Gama, Magellan, and Cabot. Students should be able to link back to these when they complete *Chapter 4: Britain abroad.*

2.1 The man who wanted to know everything serves several purposes. First and foremost it introduces the Renaissance – a key element of any serious study of the period 1509 to

Skills and processes covered in this chapter

		2.1	2.2A	2.2B
History skills	Historical enquiry			
	Using evidence and source work	✓	✓	✓
	Chronological understanding			✓
	Understanding cultural, ethnic and religious diversity	✓		
	Change and continuity	✓		✓
	Cause and consequence	✓	✓	
	Significance	✓	✓	✓
	Interpretations			
	Making links/connections	✓		
	Explores similarities and differences			
Literacy and numeracy	Key words identified/deployed	✓	✓	✓
	Extended writing			✓
	Encourages reading for meaning	✓	✓	✓
	Focuses on structuring writing			
	Asks students to use writing to explore and develop ideas			✓
	Learn through talk/discussion			
	Numeracy opportunities			
Activity types	Creative task	✓		✓
	Emphasizes role of individual			✓
	Group work			
	Independent research	✓		
	Develops study skills			

1745 (and one of the 'R' words in the title of this book!). It also looks at a true 'Renaissance man' – Leonardo da Vinci – and provides students with a window into his world. Furthermore, the lesson introduces students to the idea that a single event, invention, or even a movement, such as the Renaissance, can have far reaching consequences in both the short and the long term. Students should be able to link back to this chapter later in the book when delving into the advances made during the Enlightenment.

Lesson sequence

Lesson title	NC references	Objectives	Outcomes
2.1 The man who wanted to know everything pp34–35	Renaissance and Reformation in Europe	• Explain what is meant by the word 'renaissance'. • Examine what triggered the Renaissance. • Explore why Leonardo da Vinci was such an important 'Renaissance man'.	**All** students will summarize the information in the *Student Book*. **Most** students will carry out guided research, selecting relevant information. **Some** students will carry out independent research.
2.2A Exploring the world pp36–37 **2.2B Exploring the world pp38–39**	The first colony in America and first contact with India	• Explore what Europeans knew of the world at the beginning of the Tudor age. • Summarize why explorers were so keen to discover new routes to foreign lands. • Explain the significance of key explorers.	**All** students will summarize Columbus' voyage and discovery of the Americas. **Most** students will summarize the discoveries of a variety of Renaissance explorers. **Some** students will decide which explorer was the most significant and explain why.

Ideas for enrichment

You could counter the European joy in finding a 'new world' in the late fifteenth century by asking students to look at it from the perspective of the people who were already there. They could research the impact of European 'discovery' in the years after 1492. You might even set the challenge of finding out what happened to the six Native Americans who were kidnapped by Columbus and brought back to Queen Isabella.

Students could undertake a research project on Leonardo da Vinci. Suggest that they list their top three favourites of his paintings, ideas, or inventions. They must be able to justify their choices.

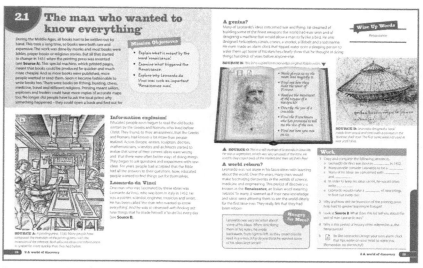

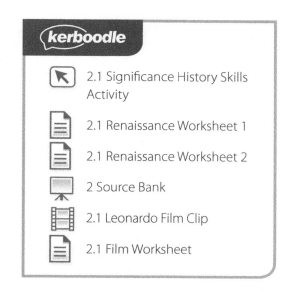

Renaissance, Revolution and Reformation pages 34–35

Lesson summary

Students will summarize and select relevant information in order to create a mind-map about the Renaissance.

What are the lesson outcomes?

All students will summarize the information in the *Student Book*.

Most students will carry out guided research, selecting relevant information.

Some students will carry out independent research.

Starter suggestion

- Students could be asked to make a list of things that they and their families use the Internet for, such as social networking, finding directions, looking up information, or emailing people. They should then consider how people did each activity before the Internet was invented. The parallel between the development of the Internet and the invention of the printing press is made in the *Student Book* and this can be explored during this starter activity.

Main learning suggestions and assessment

What activities will take place?

Task 1: Students should read pages 34–35 and create a mind-map to summarize the developments and discoveries of the Renaissance.

Task 2: Students should then use the Internet and/or the school library to research these ideas further and add more information to their mind-map.

Task 3: Students should watch 2.1 Leonardo Film Clip and complete the accompanying worksheet. They should complete either of the two 2.1 Renaissance Worksheets, in one of which, students must design an alarm clock without using electricity!

How will students demonstrate their understanding?

By creating a mind-map, students will demonstrate their ability to summarize and select relevant information. These are vital skills when completing a historical enquiry.

Plenary suggestions

- The class could play 'bowling'. In this game, one student comes to the front of the class. The rest of the students are each given paper or mini-whiteboards, and a topic. They write down a short answer (one-word answers work best) and stand up. The student at the front then has up to one minute to give as many answers as they can. If they say the same answer as a student has given, that student must sit down. The winner is the last student(s) standing, or the contestant if they 'knock down' everyone. Topics could include: Leonardo's inventions; scientific developments of the Renaissance; types of books that the printing press could print.

Differentiation suggestions

Support

- In **Task 1** lower ability students could be given a list of topics to include on their mind-map, such as medicine, religion, exploration, science, art, or Leonardo da Vinci.

Extension: Hungry for more?

- Students could make a list of the things that Leonardo da Vinci discovered and invented. They could even produce their list backwards and written from right to left like he did!

- Students could complete 2.1 Significance History Skills Activity, which focuses on the importance of the printing press in spreading new ideas.

2.2A Exploring the world

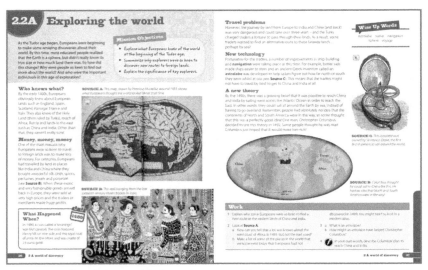

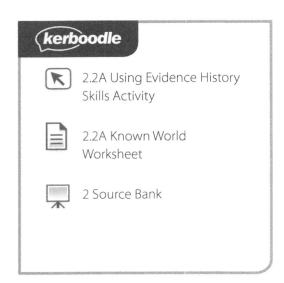

Renaissance, Revolution and Reformation pages 36–37

Lesson summary
Students will answer questions to explain what Europeans knew about the world at the beginning of the era and why they wanted to develop new routes to destinations such as China and India.

What are the lesson outcomes?
All students will summarize Columbus' voyage and discovery of the Americas.

Most students will summarize the discoveries of a variety of Renaissance explorers.

Some students will decide which explorer was the most significant and explain why.

Starter suggestion
- Students should study the map drawn by Henricus Martellus in 1489 (**Source A** on page 36) and 'spot the difference' between this and the world as we know it today. You might like to display this image on your whiteboard via the source bank for this chapter.

Main learning suggestions and assessment
What activities will take place?
Task 1: Students should read pages 36–37 and then complete Work activities **1–4** to demonstrate their understanding. They could also complete 2.2A Known World Worksheet, which includes a research-based extension task on Columbus.

Task 2: Students should create a poster advertising a competition to discover a new route to China and India. On this they should explain why a new route would be beneficial, and include any theories that they have about a new route.

Task 3: Students should complete 2.2A Using Evidence History Skills Activity, which asks them to consider Francis Drake's astrolabe.

How will students demonstrate their understanding?
In **Task 1**, the Work activities will allow students to demonstrate their abilities to make inferences from sources and to explain their ideas. The poster created in **Task 2** allows students to develop creativity and summarizing skills, as well as considering significance.

Plenary suggestions
- Students could pretend that they are interviewing Columbus for a news programme and present a short piece of drama in which Columbus explains what he is hoping to achieve and why.

Differentiation suggestions
Support
- When reading through pages 36–37 of the *Student Book*, the class could be directed towards the information they will need to complete the Work activities. Whole-class discussions could be used to help students work out answers where they have to make inferences.

- In **Task 2** a template could be produced to help students decide what information to include in their poster.

Extension: Hungry for more?
- Christopher Columbus is introduced in this lesson and will be the focus of the next lesson. Students could be asked to find out about his life before he discovered the Americas in 1492. They could then use this information to create a biography or a fact file about him.

2.2B Exploring the world

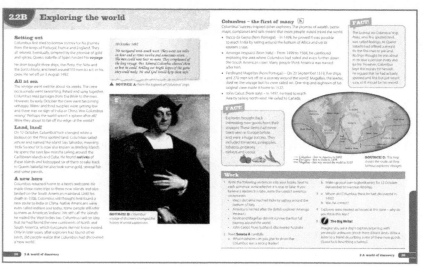

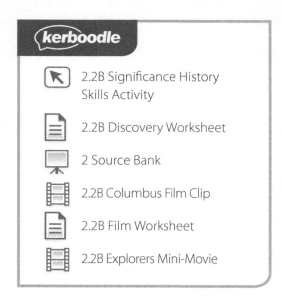

kerboodle

- 2.2B Significance History Skills Activity
- 2.2B Discovery Worksheet
- 2 Source Bank
- 2.2B Columbus Film Clip
- 2.2B Film Worksheet
- 2.2B Explorers Mini-Movie

Renaissance, Revolution and Reformation pages 38–39

Lesson summary

Students will develop a sense of chronology and summarize information to create a cartoon storyboard detailing the voyage of Columbus. They will then describe and explain the significance of other key Renaissance explorers.

What are the lesson outcomes?

All students will summarize Columbus' voyage and discovery of the Americas.

Most students will summarize the discoveries of a variety of Renaissance explorers.

Some students will decide which explorer was the most significant and explain why.

Starter suggestion

- To get students thinking about significance, they could be shown images of modern celebrities, sports personalities, and politicians, and asked which is the most important and why.

Main learning suggestions and assessment

What activities will take place?

Task 1: Students should read on pages 38–39 and create a cartoon storyboard telling the story of Columbus' discovery of the Americas.

Task 2: Students should then create a table summarizing the discoveries of other Renaissance explorers, with headings as follows: Name; Nationality; Date of discovery; Discovery; Importance of discovery (score out of 10). 2.2B Significance History Skills Activity provides an alternative way of completing this task.

Task 3: Students should use the table they have created in **Task 2** to decide which explorer was the most important. They should write a speech to give at an awards ceremony before presenting a prize to their chosen explorer.

How will students demonstrate their understanding?
Task 1 allows students to summarize information. **Task 2** encourages students to compare the achievements of different explorers in order to decide which was most important, and in **Task 3** they will explain their ideas.

Plenary suggestions

- Students could move to different areas of the classroom in order to show which explorer they think was most significant. Individuals could then be asked to explain their decision.

- Students could complete 2.2B Discovery Worksheet, perhaps as homework. This worksheet checks understanding by asking students to identify and correct false statements.

Differentiation suggestions

Support

- In **Task 1** lower ability students could be given a storyboard with captions already written in, or a a list of captions to sort into chronological order and stick onto their storyboard before illustrating it.

Extension: Hungry for more?

- Students could create an advert for some of the 'new' goods discovered by Columbus and the other explorers.

- Students could watch 2.2B Columbus Film Clip and 2.2B Explorers Mini-Movie and then complete 2.2B Film Worksheet.

Overview:
Chapter 3 Life in Tudor times

Helping you deliver KS3 History National Curriculum

The aim here is to investigate British society in the sixteenth and seventeenth centuries by looking at various aspects of life – education, the structure of society, crime and punishment, theatre, fashion, entertainment, and so on. Students will have several opportunities to use writing to explore and develop their ideas, and to organize and structure their thoughts in order to write an extended answer. They will need to read for meaning, argue for or against a particular point of view, and examine why different people promote different versions of events.

The Big Picture

Why are we teaching 'Life in Tudor times'?

'Life in…' chapters of a book serve as extremely useful all-encompassing sections when writing about a period. If there is something that I know will engage students or make them feel a connection, but won't easily fit into another chapter, then I know I can place it here! This chapter allows students to uncover the minutiae of ordinary life – which are often the things that resonate most with them. The topics are wide-ranging – from school to fashion to torture – and they provide the colour, sights, sounds, and smells of the period. This chapter is often the most successful in the classroom.

Skills and processes covered in this chapter

		3.1A	3.1B	3.2	3.3A	3.3B	3.4	3.5	3.6	3.7	3.8A	3.8B	3.9
History skills	Historical enquiry			✓	✓	✓		✓					
	Using evidence and source work	✓	✓	✓	✓	✓		✓		✓		✓	✓
	Chronological understanding									✓			
	Understanding cultural, ethnic and religious diversity	✓	✓	✓	✓	✓					✓	✓	
	Change and continuity				✓	✓			✓	✓		✓	
	Cause and consequence					✓					✓	✓	
	Significance						✓						
	Interpretations							✓					
	Making links/connections			✓		✓	✓		✓				
	Explores similarities and differences	✓	✓	✓	✓				✓	✓		✓	
Literacy and numeracy	Key words identified/deployed	✓	✓	✓	✓		✓	✓	✓		✓	✓	✓
	Extended writing		✓	✓		✓		✓		✓		✓	
	Encourages reading for meaning	✓	✓	✓	✓	✓		✓	✓	✓		✓	
	Focuses on structuring writing		✓										
	Asks students to use writing to explore and develop ideas		✓		✓		✓	✓	✓			✓	✓
	Learn through talk/discussion			✓			✓	✓	✓		✓	✓	
	Numeracy opportunities									✓			
Activity types	Creative task			✓		✓	✓		✓			✓	✓
	Emphasizes role of individual						✓	✓				✓	
	Group work												
	Independent research			✓		✓			✓				
	Develops study skills		✓					✓					

Lesson sequence

Lesson title	NC references	Objectives	Outcomes
3.1A Who's who? pp40–41 3.1B Who's who? pp42–43	Society, economy and culture across the period	• Identify the four main groups that made up Tudor society. • Categorize a variety of different historical sources.	**All** students will identify the different Tudor classes. **Most** students will describe what life was like for members of each class, using evidence from sources to support their ideas. **Some** students will explain how economic factors influenced diversity in the lives of different classes in Tudor society.
3.2 What were Tudor schools like? pp44–45	Society, economy and culture across the period	• Recall at least five facts about education in Tudor England. • Compare today's schools with those in Tudor times.	**All** students will describe a typical Tudor school day. **Most** students will be able to describe what has changed and what has stayed the same. **Some** students will be able to explain which changes are considered positive and whether they feel that anything might be worse today.
3.3A How did people have fun in Tudor times? pp46–47 3.3B How did people have fun in Tudor times? pp48–49	Society, economy and culture across the period	• Examine how and why Tudor entertainment differed from the types of entertainment we enjoy today.	**All** students will identify some Tudor pastimes. **Most** students will compare Tudor pastimes to the ways in which we have fun today. **Some** students will demonstrate their chronological understanding of the Tudor era by explaining the key characteristics of Tudor pastimes.
3.4 And now for your Shakespeare lesson... pp50–51	Society, economy and culture across the period	• Explore how the theatre became popular in Tudor times. • Explain why William Shakespeare became the most famous Englishman in the world.	**All** students will describe the achievements of William Shakespeare in the Tudor theatre. **Most** students will explain why Shakespeare became the most famous Englishman in the world. **Some** students will make links between their historical knowledge and their studies in English to explain Shakespeare's success and achievements.
3.5 Shakespeare or Fakespeare? pp52–53	Society, economy and culture across the period	• Investigate the debate into who actually wrote Shakespeare's plays and poems. • Decide whether you are a Stratfordian or an anti-Stratfordian.	**All** students will categorize evidence into whether it was written by Stratfordians or anti-Stratfordians. **Most** students will explain evidence on at least one side of the argument. **Some** students will analyse evidence on both sides of the argument to explain their final conclusion.
3.6 Fashion victims pp54–55	Society, economy and culture across the period	• Describe what some rich Tudor women did to their skin to create the 'perfect face' and why.	**All** students will identify Tudor make-up techniques. **Most** students will describe Tudor make-up techniques and the dangers they posed. **Some** students will explain how Tudor make-up trends were dangerous and draw parallels to some modern trends.
3.7 Come dine with me! pp56–57	Society, economy and culture across the period	• Investigate how and why our modern daily routine differs from that of people in Tudor times.	**All** students will describe a typical Tudor diet. **Most** students will compare the daily routines and diet of the rich and poor in Tudor times. **Some** students will compare the daily routines of different Tudor classes to our routines own today.
3.8A Crimewatch pp58–59 3.8B Crimewatch pp60–61	Society, economy and culture across the period	• Investigate how some of the poorer people in Tudor times tried to make money. • Explain why these so-called 'sturdy beggars' were treated so brutally. • Judge how well Tudor society dealt with the poor.	**All** students will describe different types of sturdy beggars. **Most** students will explain why there were so many paupers in Tudor times. **Some** students will explain what was done to punish and/or support paupers.
3.9 What did the Scottish boot, the Judas cradle and the Spanish donkey have in common? pp62–63	Society, economy and culture across the period	• Analyse why and how torture was used during the Tudor and Stuart period.	**All** students will describe the different types of torture used in Tudor times. **Most** students will explain why torture was used. **Some** students will analyse media interpretations of the use of torture.

Ideas for enrichment

In our experience, the Shakespeare or Fakespeare? debate rarely produces a consensus. Divide the class into Stratfordians and anti-Stratfordians and conduct a class debate. You can then set students the challenge of finding more evidence to back up their position using the Internet.

When studying *3.8 Crimewatch*, ask the students to pick a crime – such as 'speeding in a car', 'drink-driving', 'shoplifting', or even 'murder' – and research how the punishment for the crime has changed, evolved, hardened or softened over the years.

Students could carry out a research project on the history of their own school. They could include when it was founded, how it has changed over the years, what has stayed the same and whether there are any famous ex-students.

Ask students to look at life today. Use a recent census (from 2001 or 2011) and ask students to mind-map or write an essay on modern life and then compare and contrast it to life in Tudor England.

Use pages 56 and 57 to write a two-day diary. One day should be 'A day in the life of a Tudor' and the other day should be 'A day in the life of someone today'.

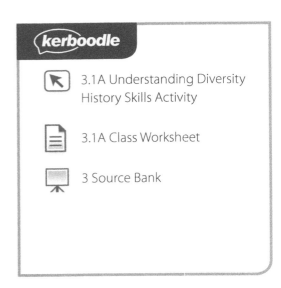

Renaissance, Revolution and Reformation pages 40–41

Lesson summary

Students consider what made people's experiences different in the Tudor era, and use a source to make inferences regarding the different classes. This lesson includes cross-curricular links to English and Drama.

What are the lesson outcomes?

All students will identify the different Tudor classes.

Most students will describe what life was like for members of each class, using evidence from sources to support their ideas.

Some students will explain how economic factors influenced diversity in the lives of different classes in Tudor society.

Starter suggestion

- Students should complete the first part of 3.1A Understanding Diversity History Skills Activity. In this activity students need to consider the factors that make people's experiences different, such as economic situation, nationality, education, or religious beliefs. Alternatively, the activity can be completed by providing a list of factors for students to write out in their chosen order.

Main learning suggestions and assessment

What activities will take place?

Task 1: Students should read pages 40–41 and then label features of each home on printed images of these houses, or similar buildings.

Task 2: As a class, work out what type of person would have lived in each house. 3.1A Understanding Diversity History Skills Activity can be used to debrief this and 3.1A Class Worksheet provides a table for students to fill in.

Task 3: Students should pretend that they are researchers for 'Through the Keyhole'. They must create a television show in which the contestants listen as the presenter describes a house and then guess what type of person the house belongs to.

Task 4: Students should create a diary entry for a typical day for someone belonging to one of the Tudor classes.

How will students demonstrate their understanding?

In **Tasks 1** and **2** students break down the components of a visual source in order to enquire about the bigger picture. In **Task 3** students will be able to consider how the lives of the different classes were different, as reflected in their homes. In **Task 4** students make inferences about what people's lives were like in the Tudor era, based on their prior knowledge.

Plenary suggestions

- Students could decide on the characteristics of a good piece of historical drama and then use these to assess each performance and set targets for improvement.

Differentiation suggestions

Support

- In **Task 1** lower ability students could be given pre-written labels to annotate the images with.

- In **Task 2** students could be given a list of questions to answer in their television shows.

Extension: Hungry for more?

- Students could complete 3.1A Understanding Diversity History Skills Activity by discussing whether economic background was the single most important factor in causing diversity in Tudor society.

- Students could complete a piece of extended writing around the above question, as homework.

3.1B Who's who?

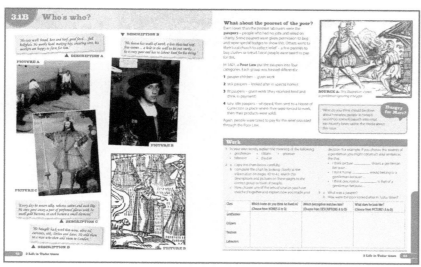

Renaissance, Revolution and Reformation pages 42-43

kerboodle

3.1B Understanding Diversity History Skills Activity

3.1B Paupers Worksheet

3 Source Bank

Lesson summary

Students will consider the diverse experiences of people living in Tudor England by matching sources to build a picture of what life was like for each class.

What are the lesson outcomes?

All students will identify the different Tudor classes.

Most students will describe what life was like for members of each class, using evidence from sources to support their ideas.

Some students will explain how economic factors influenced diversity in the lives of different classes in Tudor society.

Starter suggestion

- Students could complete Work activity **1** on page 43. This will help them consolidate their knowledge from the previous lesson by defining the key words: gentleman; citizen; yeoman; labourer; pauper.

Main learning suggestions and assessment

What activities will take place?

Task 1: Students should read pages 42–43 and then complete Work activities **2–3** or 3.1B Paupers Worksheet. They will need to refer to their learning from the previous lesson to complete these activities.

Task 2: Students should pretend that they work for a company called 'Historical Holidays', which specializes in time travelling. They have been tasked to write a travel guide for the Tudor era and must explain what types of people their clients might meet on their time travels. They should also explain what types of homes they might see and how to avoid being put into a House of Correction. There will

be opportunities for students to add additional pages to this travel guide throughout this chapter, so it should be produced on A4 paper, rather than within students' exercise books.

Task 3: Students should add a 'Tudor-English' dictionary to their travel guide in which they explain the meaning of the 'Wise Up Words' on page 43.

Task 4 Students could complete 3.1B Understanding Diversity History Skills Activity, where they consider the nature of diversity in the Tudor era. They do this by considering the aspects of life that got better for some people, but not for others. This could lead students to write an essay analysing the extent to which people's lives improved in the Tudor era.

How will students demonstrate their understanding?

Students will select and use evidence from a variety of sources in order to work out what life was like for different classes in Tudor society.

Plenary suggestions

- Students could play 'snap' with the homes, descriptions and people from pages 40–42 on printed pieces of paper.

Differentiation suggestions

Support

- In **Task 2** students could create a piece of drama in which they present a holiday show and interview some 'locals'.

Extension: Hungry for more?

- As part of the KS3 History National Curriculum for 2014, students have to complete a local history study. This unit could be an ideal opportunity to complete this requirement by studying a local Tudor home.

3.2 What were Tudor schools like?

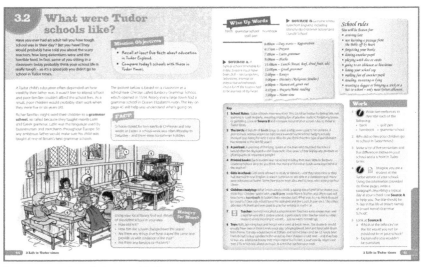

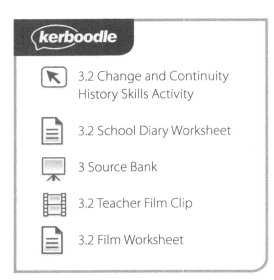

Renaissance, Revolution and Reformation pages 44–45

Lesson summary

Students will consider change and continuity when they compare a typical Tudor school day with their own, and will consider why change has occurred and how much progress there has been.

What are the lesson outcomes?

All students will describe a typical Tudor school day.

Most students will be able to describe what has changed and what has stayed the same.

Some students will be able to explain which changes are considered positive and whether they feel that anything might be worse today.

Starter suggestion

●   Students could be asked to write five social networking posts describing their week at school (one for each day). They have only 140 characters in which to identify the main features and their favourite and least favourite parts of school life! Include some rules in this activity, such as not writing personal comments about other people.

Main learning suggestions and assessment

What activities will take place?

Task 1: Students should read pages 44–45 and then complete Work activities **1–5** and 3.2 School Diary Worksheet.

Task 2: Students should pretend that the Internet existed in Tudor times, and create a website for a Tudor school. They should include pages on: the school day; school rules (and punishments!); subjects studied; the school ethos.

●   **Task 3:** Students should imagine that they have been asked to write a report for the Minister for Education. The minister wants to decide whether schools today would

benefit from any features of a Tudor school. Their reports should include: a brief description of school life; a section on recommended changes that would benefit modern schools; a section explaining any features that should not be introduced and why they were a bad idea.

Task 4: Students should watch 3.2 Teacher Film Clip and complete 3.2 Film Worksheet.

How will students demonstrate their understanding?

In **Tasks 1** and **2** students describe key features of a Tudor school, and identify change and continuity between schools then and now. In **Task 3** students make judgments about the changes that have occurred – whether they are examples of progression or regression.

Plenary suggestions

●   Students could take part in a 'hotseat' activity in which one of them is a Tudor teacher at parents' evening. He or she must respond to the 'parents' (the rest of the class), who ask questions about how their child is progressing and what school is like.

Differentiation suggestions

Support

●   In **Task 1**, a support sheet could be produced for lower ability students on which they are offered multiple-choice answers for Work activities **1–3**.

●   For **Task 2**, students could be given a template sheet with sections of the website to complete.

Extension: Hungry for more?

●   Students could complete 3.2 Change and Continuity History Skills Activity. In this activity they consider the parallels and differences between Tudor and modern schools, and then make judgments regarding how positive the changes have been.

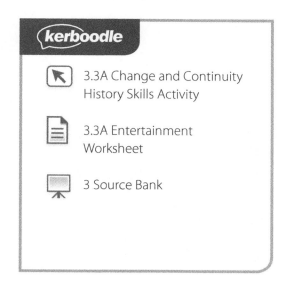

Renaissance, Revolution and Reformation pages 46–47

Lesson summary

Students will learn about Tudor pastimes and create an advert and/or a travel guide explaining the key characteristics of Tudor pastimes.

What are the lesson outcomes?

All students will identify some Tudor pastimes.

Most students will compare Tudor pastimes to the ways in which we have fun today.

Some students will demonstrate their chronological understanding of the Tudor era by explaining the key characteristics of Tudor pastimes.

Starter suggestion

- Students could complete 3.3A Change and Continuity History Skills Activity about the pastimes that we still have today. This could be completed as a group on an interactive whiteboard or individually on computers or tablets.

- Alternatively, students could be asked to make a list of the ways in which they spend their free time today. They should highlight the ones that they think people living in the Tudor era may also have enjoyed.

Main learning suggestions and assessment

What activities will take place?

Task 1: Students should complete Work activities **1** and **2** on page 47.

Task 2: Students should pretend that they are on a committee organizing a town or village fair. They have to create an advertisement telling people what events and activities will take place at the fair. This could be a poster or a leaflet.

Task 3: Students should complete 3.3A Entertainment Worksheet, which focuses on the 'Cotswolds Olimpick Games'.

Task 4: In *3.1B Who's who?* students created a travel guide for 'Historical Holidays'. They should now add another section to this guide, explaining what pastimes tourists could get involved in during the Tudor era.

How will students demonstrate their understanding?

In the KS3 History National Curriculum for 2014 there is reference to students demonstrating their understanding of chronology by explaining key trends and characteristics of an era. In this lesson they will demonstrate their ability to explain how people spent their free time. **Task 1** will also enable students to develop the skill of analysing change and continuity.

Plenary suggestions

- Students could write a 'recipe' for the perfect weekend in Tudor times. What pastimes would they include?

Differentiation suggestions

Support

- In **Task 4** lower ability students could be given a template. This could include boxes about three pastimes for students to complete, rather than trying to describe and explain all those considered in the *Student Book*.

Extension: Hungry for more?

- To connect the learning from this lesson to that of the next, students could be asked to research some of the concepts that they will be studying. For example, they could research where the word 'holiday' comes from and find out when Tudor people had holidays.

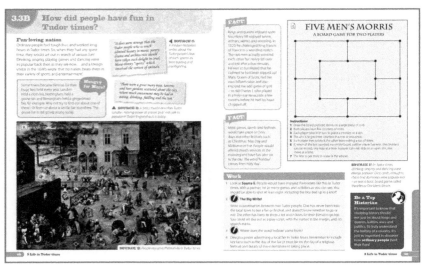

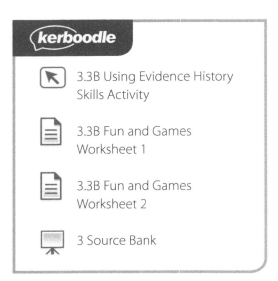

Renaissance, Revolution and Reformation pages 48–49

Lesson summary

Students will learn about Tudor pastimes and create an advert and/or a travel guide explaining the key characteristics of Tudor pastimes.

What are the lesson outcomes?

All students will identify some Tudor pastimes.

Most students will compare Tudor pastimes to the ways in which we have fun today.

Some students will demonstrate their chronological understanding of the Tudor era by explaining the key characteristics of Tudor pastimes.

Starter suggestion

● Students could make their own wordsearch about Tudor pastimes, choosing key words based on the learning that took place in the previous lesson. Grids could be produced for students to use and they should aim to include up to ten words.

Main learning suggestions and assessment

What activities will take place?

Task 1: Using the information on pages 46–47, students should be asked to create 'Top Trumps' cards for the different pastimes that Tudors enjoyed. The criteria to judge each sport could be decided by the class, but they should include a category entitled 'would people enjoy this today', to encourage students to consider change and continuity and prepare them for the next tasks.

Task 2: Students should complete 3.3B Using Evidence History Skills Activity in which they break down **Source E** from the *Student Book* in order to evaluate how useful it is to a historian.

Task 3: Students should be given writing frames and asked to write up their ideas from **Task 2**. This task could be used as formative assessment to work out how well students have grasped the content and skills in this chapter so far.

Task 4: Students should complete Work activities **1–4** on page 49, followed by 3.3B Fun and Games Worksheet 2.

How will students demonstrate their understanding?

Students will formulate their ideas in the 'Top Trumps' cards, giving them the opportunity to compare pastimes within and beyond the Tudor era. They will develop skills in source analysis by completing 3.3B Using Evidence History Skills Activity and can formally demonstrate their understanding by completing the written activity in **Task 3**.

Plenary suggestions

● Students should be given some examples of answers from **Task 3** (these could be from the current group, a previous class, or made up) and asked to put them in order from 'good' to 'best'.

● Students could play Five Men's Morris using 3.3B Fun and Games Worksheet 1.

Differentiation suggestions

Support

● For **Task 1**, lower ability students could be given 'Top Trumps' cards where the criteria have already been created.

● For **Task 3** writing frames could be produced to support students of different abilities.

Extension: Hungry for more?

● Students could complete the 'Be a Top Historian' activity on page 49.

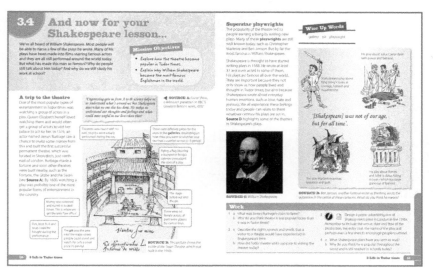

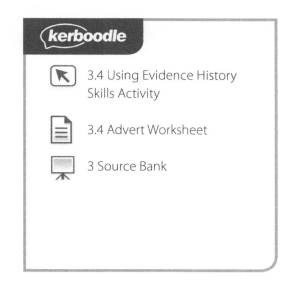

Renaissance, Revolution and Reformation pages 50–51

Lesson summary

Students will work in pairs or small groups to conduct a historical enquiry into the life and achievements of William Shakespeare. This lesson includes cross-curricular links to English.

What are the lesson outcomes?

All students will describe the achievements of William Shakespeare in Tudor theatre.

Most students will explain why Shakespeare became the most famous Englishman in the world.

Some students will make links between their historical knowledge and their studies in English to explain Shakespeare's success and achievements.

Starter suggestion

- Students could be shown a series of images associated with Shakespeare's plays and asked to link images. For example, *Julius Caesar* and *Henry V* could go together, as they are both plays about historical events.

Main learning suggestions and assessment

What activities will take place?

Task 1: Students should read pages 50–51 and complete Work activities **1–4**. 3.4 Advert Worksheet provides guidance for Work activity **3**.

Task 2: Students should design a museum exhibition about Shakespeare and why he became so famous.

Task 3: Groups of students should complete a 'speed dating' activity in which they research a Shakespeare play and think about what inferences they can make about Tudor society from it. The class can then 'speed date' – give groups two minutes with another group to swap information about the play they have researched and fill in a summary table.

Task 4: Students should pretend that they are Tudor directors putting on a play, perhaps one they are studying in English lessons. They could write a proposal for the theatre, explaining what they will need for their play and how it should be staged, including spercial effects and ticket prices.

Task 5: Students should complete 3.4 Using Evidence History Skills Activity.

How will students demonstrate their understanding?

In **Task 1** students will describe the experience of Tudor theatre-goers. In **Task 2**, students must decide on the information to include and on the language and style to present their work in order to appeal to a specific audience. They must also explain the significance of Shakespeare.

Plenary suggestions

- If students have studied the Middle Ages and the Wars of the Roses, they could think about interpretations of Richard III, and how Shakespeare portrayed him and why.

Differentiation suggestions

Support

- In **Task 3**, lower ability students could be given famous plays, such as *Romeo and Juliet*, to research.

Extension: Hungry for more?

- Students could watch a film or television programme of, or based on, one of Shakespeare's plays. They should then write a review, from Shakespeare's point of view. Would he have approved of it or not?

- For Work activity **3**, you might show higher ability students the title pages of Shakespeare's plays and ask them to think about and recreate what a Tudor playbill may have looked like.

3.5 Shakespeare or Fakespeare?

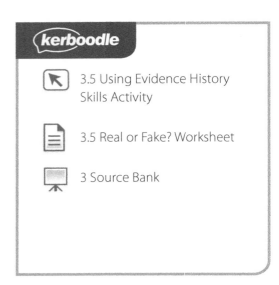

Renaissance, Revolution and Reformation pages 52–53

Lesson summary

Students will use a variety of sources to conduct a historical enquiry into whether or not William Shakespeare wrote the plays with which he is credited. This lesson includes cross-curricular links to English.

What are the lesson outcomes?

All students will categorize evidence into whether it was written by Stratfordians or anti-Stratfordians.

Most students will explain evidence on at least one side of the argument.

Some students will analyse evidence on both sides of the argument to explain their final conclusion.

Starter suggestion

- Students could consolidate their knowledge from the previous lesson by writing their own 'true or false' statements to swap with a partner.

Main learning suggestions and assessment

What activities will take place?

Task 1: Students should read pages 52–53 and then complete Work activities **1–4**. 3.5 Using Evidence History Skills Activity guides students through an analysis of some of the sources in this lesson.

Task 2: Students should develop their ideas from Work activity **2** by completing an 'evidence table' about the sources they have studied, with headings as below:

Source	Author	Shakespeare or Fakespeare?	Summary of evidence

Task 3: Students should be given a mark scheme and/ or writing frames, and asked to write an essay in which they evaluate and analyse whether or not William Shakespeare really wrote the plays that we credit him with. This activity can be used for formative assessment.

Task 4: Students should use the mark scheme to self- or peer-assess their work, noting what they have done well and how they could improve. They should then be given time to improve their essays.

How will students demonstrate their understanding?

Students will write an analytical essay. In this they will explain evidence for and against William Shakespeare being the author of the plays credited to him.

Plenary suggestions

- The class could vote on 'Shakespeare or Fakespeare' and explain their decisions orally.

Differentiation suggestions

Support

- For Work activity **2** kinaesthetic learners could use 3.5 Real or Fake? Worksheet, which has copies of the sources that they can stick into the correct columns, rather than writing details out.

- In **Task 2**, students could be asked to consider a small number of the sources, rather than all of them. The first two columns of the table could be completed with the source reference and author.

Extension: Hungry for more?

- Students could take the essay they wrote **Task 3** and use the target set for them in **Task 4** to write a final version of their essay.

3.6 Fashion victims

Renaissance, Revolution and Reformation pages 54–55

Lesson summary

Students will create a magazine article and/or a piece of drama offering hints and tips to Tudor women and exposing the 'Make-Up Cover-Up!' This lesson includes cross-curricular links to PSHE (body image; cultural influences) and Chemistry.

What are the lesson outcomes?

All students will identify Tudor make-up techniques.

Most students will describe Tudor make-up techniques and the dangers they posed.

Some students will explain how Tudor make-up trends were dangerous and draw parallels to modern trends.

Starter suggestion

- Students could be given a copy of one of the portraits of Elizabeth I, and asked to describe her face. 3.6 Using Evidence History Skills Activity is a version of this task. It could be used to debrief the activity or it could be completed by individual students on laptops or tablets.

Main learning suggestions and assessment

What activities will take place?

Task 1: Students should read pages 54–55 and complete Work activities **1–3**.

Task 2: Students should create a magazine article offering make-up hints and tips for the Tudor fashion victim.

Task 3: Students should complete 3.6 Matching Worksheet to check their knowledge of the dangerous effects of Tudor make-up. They should then present a 'news exposé' about the Tudor make-up industry and the dangers women are facing by using fashionable make-up techniques.

How will students demonstrate their understanding?

The tasks allows students to identify, describe, and explain Tudor trends and the dangers they posed, and to draw parallels with today.

Plenary suggestions

- Give students one minute to present an advertisement on a television shopping channel, for a piece of Tudor make-up. They should explain what it does and how to use it.

Differentiation suggestions

Support

- In **Task 1**, lower ability students could be given a table to complete for Work question **1**, with headings as below:

Chemical/substance	Use	Effect

- It may be useful to have a blank template ready for Work activity **3** so that students can focus on the main task rather than drawing out a face.

- In **Task 2** it may be useful to model the task by having some examples of beauty magazines for students to look at. These will show them examples of how they could set out their work and what style of writing they could use.

Extension: Hungry for more?

- Students could complete the 'Hungry for More' activity on page 55.

- Students could research the chemicals used in make-up today. Can they find any ingredients as revolting as those used by the Tudors?

3.7 Come dine with me!

Renaissance, Revolution and Reformation pages 56–57

Lesson summary
Students will create a piece of drama about Tudor food and customs associated with meal times. This lesson includes cross-curricular links to English (speaking and listening).

What are the lesson outcomes?
All students will describe a typical Tudor diet.

Most students will compare the daily routines and diet of the rich and poor in Tudor times.

Some students will compare the daily routines of different Tudor classes to our own routines today.

Starter suggestion
- Students could create a 'daily routine' timeline for a typical school day, listing what they do and what food they eat.

Main learning suggestions and assessment
What activities will take place?
Task 1: Students should read pages 56–57 and use the information to complete Work activities **1** and **2**. Their opening line for activity **2** could be: 'Tonight we had the most sumptuous feast! To start with…'

Task 2: Students should script an episode of a Tudor TV show in which people go to a Tudor person's house for dinner and then judge the food, entertainment, and general experience. One host should be a country worker and the second should be a rich person. The guests could comment on the food, the house, and even the table manners of the other guests!

Task 3: Students should create their own version of **Source B** by drawing a scene of their family sitting down to dinner. They could then 'spot the difference' between the two images.

Task 4: Students should watch 3.7 Country Life Film Clip and complete 3.7 Film Worksheet. This clip features a country girl explaining her daily routine and her family's typical diet.

How will students demonstrate their understanding?
Tasks 1 and **2** will allow students to demonstrate their ability to describe how diet and daily routines differed between the rich and poor during Tudor times. **Task 3** will then extend this by allowing students to compare and contrast Tudor customs with their experiences today. These activities link to change and continuity, diversity and chronological understanding (describing characteristics within and across periods).

Plenary suggestions
- Students could repeat the starter activity, but this time creating a timeline for an average Tudor day. The class could then discuss how things have changed and why they think this is.

Differentiation suggestions
Support
- A two-circle Venn diagram could be used to help students compare and contrast the lives of country workers and the rich.

- Students could also complete 3.7 Using Evidence History Skills Activity in which they consider a rich Tudor family's diet.

Extension: Hungry for more?
- Students could complete 3.7 Etiquette Worksheet, in which they create a Tudor book of etiquette aimed at the upper classes. This would make a good homework activity.

3.8A Crimewatch

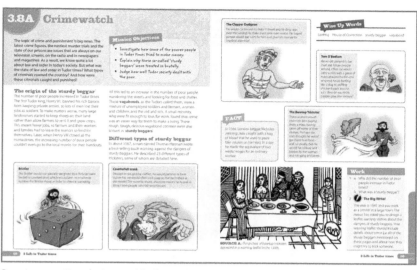

Renaissance, Revolution and Reformation pages 58–59

Lesson summary

Students will take part in a series of drama tasks, in which they explain why there are so many 'sturdy beggars', what types of tricks beggars pulled, and how they were punished. This lesson includes cross-curricular links to Drama, English (speaking and listening), and Citizenship (considering the nature of crime and the ethics behind punishment).

What are the lesson outcomes?

All students will describe different types of sturdy beggars.

Most students will explain why there were so many paupers in Tudor times.

Some students will explain what was done to punish and/or support paupers.

Starter suggestion

- Students could be told about Nicholas Jennings being arrested in 1566 with a bag of blood. Ask them to consider what they think his crime was. This can be used as a hook to get students to consider their own definition of crime as opposed to the Tudor definition.

Main learning suggestions and assessment

What activities will take place?

Task 1: Students should read pages 58–59 and complete Work activities **1** and **2**.

Task 2: Students should create an appeal for a Tudor charity that helps poor people. They should explain why so many people have fallen on hard times.

Task 3: Students should complete 3.8 Cause and Consequence History Skills Activity and 3.8A Tricksters Worksheet to check their understanding of the different types of sturdy beggar.

How will students demonstrate their understanding?

In **Tasks 1–3** students will describe and explain how some poorer Tudor people tried to make money. They will explain why there were so many paupers and what was done to punish and/or support them in the following lesson.

Plenary suggestions

- Students could be asked to 'freeze-frame' a scene in which they each take the role of a different type of sturdy beggar. When they are tapped on the shoulder they could explain what that person might be thinking, using their knowledge of why so many people were so desperate in Tudor times.

Differentiation suggestions

Support

- Peer support could be used in **Task 2** by pairing lower ability students with higher ability students.

- In Work activity **2**, lower ability students could be asked to concentrate on two or three examples of sturdy beggars rather than attempting to describe them all. You might like to show them an example of a modern warning leaflet, so they understand the format.

Extension: Hungry for more?

- Thomas Harman's book described 23 different types of tricksters. Students could be asked to research some of these and present their findings in a 'police briefing' to the rest of the class.

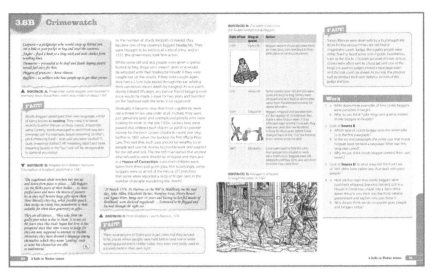

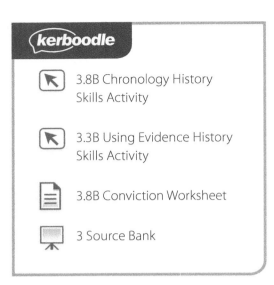

Renaissance, Revolution and Reformation pages 60–61

Lesson summary
Students will take part in a series of drama tasks, in which they explain why there are so many 'sturdy beggars', what types of tricks beggars pulled, and how they were punished. This lesson includes cross-curricular links to Drama, English (speaking and listening), and Citizenship (considering the nature of crime and the ethics behind punishment).

What are the lesson outcomes?
All students will describe different types of sturdy beggars.

Most students will explain why there were so many paupers in Tudor times.

Some students will explain what was done to punish and/or support paupers.

Starter suggestion
- Students could complete 3.8B Using Evidence History Skills Activity. This task encourages students to consider how the problem of beggars got worse during the Tudor era.

Main learning suggestions and assessment
What activities will take place?
Task 1: Students should read pages 60–61 and complete Work activities **1–4**.

Task 2: The class should prepare a 'court case' in which a judge hears the cases of five sturdy beggars (from the previous lesson) and decides how to punish each one. The class should be split into five teams, and each team should prepare the cases for and against one sturdy beggar. Every member of the class should then be assigned different roles: the five defendants; five defence lawyers; five prosecution lawyers; witnesses to be questioned; the judge; the jury.

The class can then act out the court case. It may be most appropriate for you to act as the judge, in order to organize proceedings.

Task 3: Students could then create a newspaper article relating the above court cases and detailing how and why punishments were chosen for each of the sturdy beggars.

Task 4: Students should complete 3.8B Chronology History Skills Activity, in which they identify and describe trends in the treatment of sturdy beggars across the Tudor era. 3.8B Conviction Worksheet also focuses on the changing punishments for beggars under Tudor monarchs.

How will students demonstrate their understanding?
In **Tasks 2** and **3** students will describe each type of sturdy beggar, use evidence to show two sides of an argument, and explain the different types of punishment and relief. They will also develop teamwork skills.

Plenary suggestions
- Students could be asked to consider ethical issues such as the reasons people commit crimes and whether punishments should take the form of retribution or reform.

Differentiation suggestions
Support
- Lower ability students could be given simpler tasks to perform in **Task 3**. For example, they could act as members of the jury.

Extension: Hungry for more?
- In earlier lessons in this chapter students created a travel guide for 'Historical Holidays'. They could add to this, warning travellers of the different sturdy beggars, how to avoid them, and what punishment they could expect to face if they got involved in such crimes.

3.9 What did the Scottish boot, the Judas cradle and the Spanish donkey have in common?

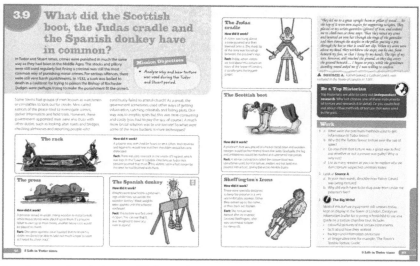

Renaissance, Revolution and Reformation pages 62–63

Lesson summary

Students will answer questions and complete creative activities in order to analyse why and how torture was used, as well as how it has been interpreted in the media.

What are the lesson outcomes?

All students will describe the different types of torture used in Tudor times.

Most students will explain why torture was used.

Some students will analyse media interpretations of the use of torture.

Starter suggestion

- Students could be told that they are researchers for a television drama about the police. Their task is to make a list of all the ways in which the police gather evidence, which would be featured on the show. Which do they think would be the most gripping for the audience?

Main learning suggestions and assessment

What activities will take place?

Task 1: Students should read pages 62–63 and complete 3.9 Notes Worksheet as they read, which will help them summarize and make notes on each kind of torture. They should then use the information to complete Work activities **1–3**. For activity 3, remind students of the conventions of a leaflet, such as text not running across the fold.

Task 2: Students should create a job description for a justice of the peace, describing all the different duties they had and explaining what personal qualities they would need.

Task 3: Students should watch 3.9 Tower Film Clip and complete 3.9 Film Worksheet. In this film clip, a Tower of London torturer explains how torture was used to get information from victims.

Task 4: Students should complete 3.9 Interpretations History Skills Activity in which they consider interpretations of the use of torture in film and television programmes and whether it turns something so gruesome into a triviality.

How will students demonstrate their understanding?

The starter activity introduces students to the idea of the purpose of a television programme, and allows them to consider a modern parallel to this topic. **Task 1** allows students to demonstrate their ability to describe the various methods of torture and to explain why they were used. In **Task 4** students consider historical interpretations of torture.

Plenary suggestions

- Students could be asked why they think torture is no longer used in Britain.

Differentiation suggestions

Support

- In **Task 2** students could be given a list of words to include in their job description. The task could also be modelled, with the whole class writing a description for a job that they are more familiar with (such as a teacher).

- The questions on 3.9 Film Worksheet are progressively more challenging to ensure that there are tasks that are accessible to students of all abilities.

Extension: Hungry for more?

- Students could put the methods of torture described on pages 62–63 in order, according to which they think was the worst. They should then explain their ideas.

Overview:
Chapter 4 Britain abroad

Helping you deliver KS3 History National Curriculum

The KS3 History National Curriculum for 2014 specifically mentions 'the first colony in America and first contact with India' in the list of example topics. This chapter explores these topics in detail and prepares students well for a return to them in later books.

Throughout the chapter students are required to use key historical terminology appropriately, and to determine the significance of both key individuals and international history. There is also a good balance between activities that require students to read for meaning, to select and combine information from sources and text to answer questions, and to use their creative skills to produce interesting and historically accurate work.

The Big Picture

Why are we teaching 'Britain abroad'?

It was during the Tudor period that the seeds of the British Empire were sown. With the requirements of the new KS3 Programme of Study in mind, we have dedicated a chapter to the early years of Britain's colonial past. The first two lessons in the chapter chart Britain's early attempts to establish colonies and trading stations in the New World and India. *4.2 How was Britain involved in the slave trade?* establishes how commerce and profit margins were the key motivating factors of Britain's growing trade in goods. We return to this topic in greater detail in the next book in the series (*Industry, Invention and Empire: Britain 1745–1901*).

Also included in this chapter is an investigation into the much-loved world of pirates and privateers. This topic is

Skills and processes covered in this chapter

		4.1A	4.1B	4.2	4.3
History skills	Historical enquiry	✓	✓		
	Using evidence and source work	✓	✓	✓	✓
	Chronological understanding		✓		✓
	Understanding cultural, ethnic and religious diversity				
	Change and continuity	✓			
	Cause and consequence	✓	✓	✓	
	Significance	✓		✓	
	Interpretations				
	Making links/connections		✓	✓	
	Explores similarities and differences				
Literacy and numeracy	Key words identified/deployed	✓	✓	✓	✓
	Extended writing		✓		✓
	Encourages reading for meaning	✓	✓	✓	✓
	Focuses on structuring writing				✓
	Asks students to use writing to explore and develop ideas	✓	✓	✓	
	Learn through talk/discussion			✓	
	Numeracy opportunities				✓
Activity types	Creative task				✓
	Emphasizes role of individual	✓	✓	✓	✓
	Group work				
	Independent research				
	Develops study skills		✓		

universally popular with young people. We study Blackbeard – the original pirate of the Caribbean and one of the most infamous pirates of all – and put him and his fellow pirates and privateers firmly in the context of international trade during Tudor and Stuart times.

Lesson sequence

Lesson title	NC references	Objectives	Outcomes
4.1A How did Britain build an empire? pp64–65 **4.1B How did Britain build an empire? pp66–67**	The first colony in America and first contact with India	• Explore how and why the British Empire began. • Examine the significance of key individuals in the growth of the British Empire.	**All** students will summarize information to describe events that helped to build the British Empire. **Most** students will explain how one individual was significant in the creation of the British Empire. **Some** students will analyse factors that led to the creation of the British Empire, deciding which were the most significant.
4.2 How was Britain involved in the slave trade? pp68–69	Society, economy and culture across the period	• Recall why slaves were taken to the New World. • Examine Britain's role in the slave trade.	**All** students will describe the triangular slave trade. **Most** students will explain how Britain benefitted from the slave trade. **Some** students will analyse whether or not Britain should apologize for its involvement in the slave trade.
4.3 Blackbeard: the original pirate of the Caribbean pp70–71	Society, economy and culture across the period	• Explain the difference between a pirate and a privateer. • Explain why monarchs encouraged privateers. • Recall key events in Blackbeard's life.	**All** students will describe the life and times of Blackbeard. **Most** students will create a historical interpretation by using evidence to present Blackbeard as a hero or a villain. **Some** students will analyse historical interpretations to explain why they exist and how useful they are to historians.

Ideas for enrichment

Students could research which parts of the British Empire still exist, where in the world they are, and the history of their connections with Britain. This chapter also lends itself well to comparison projects. For example, ask students to research slavery or piracy today. Piracy could also be the focus for a class project. For example, students could research a different pirate or privateer such as William Kidd, Black Bart, Anne Bonny, or Henry Morgan (of Captain Morgan rum fame!).

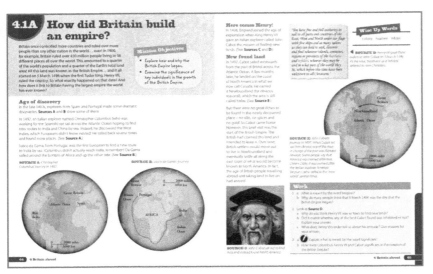

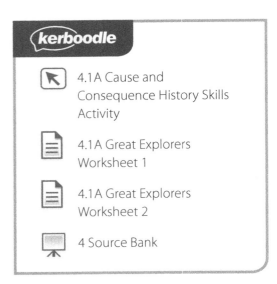

Renaissance, Revolution and Reformation pages 64–65

Lesson summary

Students will assess the significance of individual explorers in the creation of the British Empire by working in groups to create a campaign. This lesson includes cross-curricular links to English (speaking and listening).

What are the lesson outcomes?

All students will summarize information to describe events that helped to build the British Empire.

Most students will explain how one individual was significant in the creation of the British Empire.

Some students will analyse factors that led to the creation of the British Empire, deciding which were the most significant.

Starter suggestion

- Students could be asked to define key words that will be vital in this chapter, such as: empire; colony; colonization; explorer; economic. They could research their own definitions using a dictionary, or be given a linking lines task.

Main learning suggestions and assessment

What activities will take place?

Task 1: Students should read pages 64–65 and use the information to complete Work activities **1–3** and 4.1A Great Explorers Worksheet 1.

Task 2: Students should consider the significance of Christopher Columbus, Vasco da Gama, and John Cabot, and their roles in the creation of the British Empire. Students should be split into small groups. Each group must decide which explorer to nominate for the 'most significant explorer' prize, and put together the case for their chosen individual. Their campaign could include speeches, posters, and

badges. The class should then decide on success criteria for the presentations, and each group could assess another group and offer them feedback.

Task 3: Students should complete 4.1A Cause and Consequence History Skills Activity, in which they analyse the factors that made Britain want an empire.

How will students demonstrate their understanding?

In **Tasks 1** and **2** students will summarize events that led to the creation of the British Empire. **Task 2** allows students to explain the contribution of an individual explorer and demonstrate their ability to explain this significance. In **Task 3** students start to analyse the significance of other factors in the establishment of the British Empire.

Plenary suggestions

- Students could continue the 'most significant explorer' theme by casting their votes on a ballot slip and explaining their choice.

- Students could complete 4.1A Great Explorers 2, in which they design a memorial for the explorer they deem most significant.

Differentiation suggestions

Support

- Peer support could be used in **Task 2.** Differentiation by task could take the form of allocating specific explorers to certain groups. For example, students studied Columbus in some depth in chapter 2, so lower ability students could focus on him.

Extension: Hungry for more?

- Students could write a letter to one of the contenders in the competition, explaining why they did not win the title of 'most significant explorer'. They should compare and contrast the explorers studied in this lesson.

4.1B How did Britain build an empire?

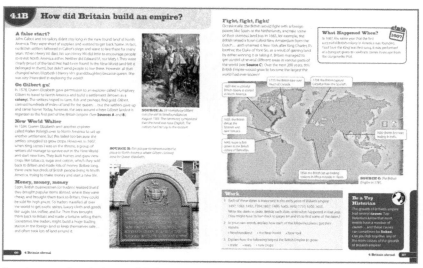

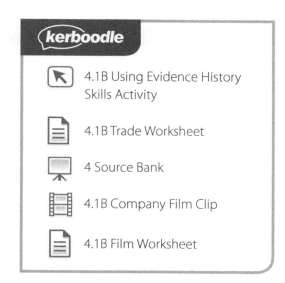

Renaissance, Revolution and Reformation pages 66–67

4.1B How did Britain build an empire?

Lesson summary
Students will assess the significance of factors that led to the creation of the British Empire by summarizing information to create a cartoon storyboard.

What are the lesson outcomes?
All students will summarize information to describe events that helped to build the British Empire.

Most students will explain how one individual was significant in the creation of the British Empire.

Some students will analyse factors that led to the creation of the British Empire, deciding which were the most significant.

Starter suggestion
- Students could be shown a copy of **Source A** on page 66 and asked what they think it shows. They could do this by first breaking down the image by playing 'I spy' to identify five features of the source. Then they should use their own knowledge from the previous lesson to put the source in context.

Main learning suggestions and assessment
What activities will take place?
Task 1: Students should read pages 66–67 and use the information to complete Work activities **1–3**.

Task 2: Students should create a cartoon storyboard explaining how the Empire developed by selecting the individuals and events that they feel are most significant.

Task 3: Following the creation of their cartoon storyboard, students should then write a paragraph explaining what they feel the most significant event or individual was, and why.

Task 4: Students should watch 4.1B Company Film Clip and then complete 4.1B Film Worksheet. This clip features a soldier explaining how the East India Company traded.

How will students demonstrate their understanding?
Tasks 1 and **2** will enable students to describe the development of the British Empire and to explain the role of individuals. In **Task 3** students will decide what the most significant factor was and explain this.

Plenary suggestions
- Students could pretend to be Elizabeth I, about to knight Walter Raleigh for his contributions to the country. They should prepare and give a short speech explaining why he is to be knighted.

- Students could complete 4.1B Using Evidence History Skills Activity. In this task, students analyse a sales catalogue from the East India Company in order to help them work with evidence and make inferences from a source.

Differentiation suggestions
Support
- In **Task 2**, lower ability students could be given captions to stick onto their storyboard in the correct order (with some extras to omit!).

Extension: Hungry for more?
- Students could be asked to research the East India Company and its contribution to the British Empire. They could then use 4.1B Trade Worksheet to write a letter convincing someone else to join the company and explaining the benefits of doing so.

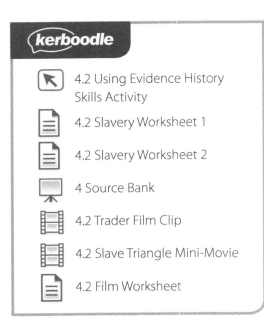

Renaissance, Revolution and Reformation pages 68–69

Lesson summary

Students will examine why Britain became involved in the slave trade and decide whether or not Britain should apologize for its involvement.

What are the lesson outcomes?

All students will describe the triangular slave trade.

Most students will explain how Britain benefitted from the slave trade.

Some students will analyse whether or not Britain should apologize for its involvement in the slave trade.

Starter suggestion

- Students could be given examples of the use of slaves throughout history and asked to put them into chronological order.

Main learning suggestions and assessment

What activities will take place?

Task 1: Students should read pages 68–69 and watch 4.2 Slave Triangle Mini-Movie. They should then complete Work activities **1–5** and 4.2 Slavery Worksheet 1.

Task 2: Students should complete 4.2 Using Evidence History Skills Activity and then list the effects of slavery and categorize these into 'positive' or 'negative'.

Task 3: Students should then be asked whether Britain should apologize for its involvement in the slave trade. They could consider the reasons why it began; how Britain benefitted from it; who else was involved; and the humanitarian cost. Students should then write to the prime minister explaining their opinion.

Task 4: Students should watch 4.2 Trader Film Clip and then complete 4.2 Film Worksheet.

How will students demonstrate their understanding?

In **Task 3** students will explain why the slave trade began and consider whether the economic advantages outweighed the humanitarian cost.

Plenary suggestions

- Students could play key word bingo. A list of key words should be shared (around 12). Students should chose nine of these, and write them into a three-by-three grid. You, or a student, should then give clues to each key word so that the contestants can cross them off in their grid. They need to achieve a line or a full house.

Differentiation suggestions

Support

- In **Task 2**, lower ability students could be given a set of 'effects' cards to categorize so that the activity becomes a kinaesthetic one.

- In **Task 3** students could be given a writing frame which includes key questions to answer.

Extension: Hungry for more?

- Students could research how the slave trade benefitted Britain, by examining an area associated with it. For example, students could research: a stately home owned by someone who profited from slavery, such as Harewood House in Leeds; or the homes of merchants and warehouses in towns such as Liverpool, Hull, and Bristol.

- Students could complete 4.2 Slavery Worksheet 2, perhaps for homework.

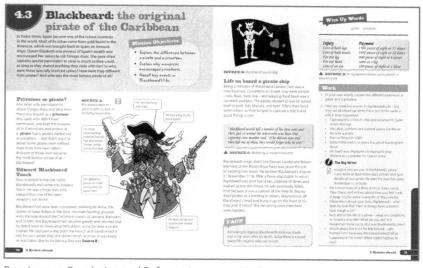

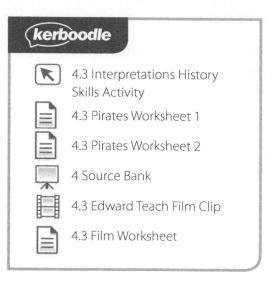

Renaissance, Revolution and Reformation pages 70–71

Lesson summary

Students will create their own historical interpretation by scripting a short film called 'The life and times of Blackbeard'. This lesson includes cross-curricular links to English (speaking and listening), Drama, and Media Studies.

What are the lesson outcomes?

All students will describe the life and times of Blackbeard.

Most students will create a historical interpretation by using evidence to present Blackbeard as a hero or a villain.

Some students will analyse historical interpretations to explain why they exist and how useful they are to historians.

Starter suggestion

- Students should be shown a paragraph that includes some 'pirate speak'. Ask them to translate it.

Main learning suggestions and assessment

What activities will take place?

Task 1: Students should be shown a short clip of a film about pirates, such as *Treasure Island* or one of the *Pirates of the Caribbean* films. Whilst watching the clip students should make two lists: one listing anything they think is historical fact; one listing words to describe the clip's interpretation of pirates.

Task 2: Students should read pages 70–71 and complete Work activities **1–3** and 4.3 Pirates Worksheet 1.

Task 3: Students should work in small groups to create new historical interpretations by scripting a short film about the life

and times of Blackbeard. Time permitting, they could also create props and costumes and perform a scene for the rest of the class.

Task 4: Students should watch 4.3 Edward Teach Film Clip and then complete 4.3 Film Worksheet.

How will students demonstrate their understanding?

Task 1 can be used as an introduction to get students thinking about historical interpretations. In **Task 2** students will describe the life and times of Blackbeard. In **Task 3** students will select evidence and language to portray Blackbeard as either a hero or a villain. This demonstrates their understanding of how different interpretations arise.

Plenary suggestions

- Students could read exemplar answers to the question 'How useful are films like *Pirates of the Caribbean* to historians studying pirates?' They should be given a mark scheme and asked to put three or four answers in order of how good they are.

Differentiation suggestions

Support

- In **Task 3** students could be given suggestions of scenes to include. This will help them to organize their ideas and to decide what detail to include. If students are too shy to act out their films, why not ask them to make and use sock puppets?

Extension: Hungry for more?

- Students could complete 4.3 Interpretations History Skills Activity in which they develop an understanding of historical interpretations by deciding whether Sir Francis Drake was a pirate or a privateer.

- Students could complete 4.3 Pirates Worksheet 2, perhaps as homework.

Overview:
Chapter 5 Queen Elizabeth

Helping you deliver KS3 History National Curriculum

The ups and downs of Princess Elizabeth's life mirror Britain's ups and downs during the English Reformation and Counter Reformation at the time of Henry VIII, Edward VI, and Mary I. Elizabeth's rocky road to monarchy is charted, as well as the conflict she encountered with foreign powers, particularly Spain. This is highlighted in the *5.4 Match of the day: England versus Spain* lessons. Students will be challenged to use a wide range of historical skills, such as selecting and combining information from sources and text to answer questions, and evaluating the causes of events. They will have the opportunity to make links between different events and changes and show how one event or change could lead to another. Students will be required to use writing to explore and develop ideas as well as organize and structure text in order to write an extended answer.

The Big Picture

Why are we teaching 'Queen Elizabeth'?

The reign of Elizabeth I is so iconic and of such importance that we decided it deserved a chapter to itself. Since students often engage most with the historical figures that they can relate to, the first lesson begins by looking at Elizabeth when she was the same age as the students. This lesson engages the students, informs them about the life and education of a wealthy girl during this period, and allows them to infer the qualities needed to become a success.

We then examine the public relations campaign that Elizabeth waged throughout her reign by examining a number of her portraits. This allows students to understand the importance of image and how monarchs were perceived. Further, *Assessing Your Learning 2* challenges students to look at the Rainbow Portrait in greater detail.

Skills and processes covered in this chapter

		5.1	5.2	5.3	5.4A	5.4B
History skills	Historical enquiry		✓		✓	✓
	Using evidence and source work	✓	✓	✓		✓
	Chronological understanding		✓			
	Understanding cultural, ethnic and religious diversity	✓		✓	✓	✓
	Change and continuity	✓	✓			
	Cause and consequence	✓		✓	✓	✓
	Significance					✓
	Interpretations		✓			
	Making links/connections					✓
	Explores similarities and differences	✓	✓		✓	
Literacy and numeracy	Key words identified/deployed			✓	✓	✓
	Extended writing					✓
	Encourages reading for meaning	✓	✓	✓	✓	✓
	Focuses on structuring writing	✓				
	Asks students to use writing to explore and develop ideas		✓	✓	✓	✓
	Learn through talk/discussion		✓	✓	✓	
	Numeracy opportunities				✓	
Activity types	Creative task	✓		✓	✓	✓
	Emphasizes role of individual				✓	✓
	Group work			✓		
	Independent research					
	Develops study skills		✓			✓

The relationship between Elizabeth and Mary, Queen of Scots, has all the drama of a soap opera and a suitably grisly end. In our experience, *5.3 Why did Queen Elizabeth kill her cousin?* is a favourite lesson of the students and they usually race each other to crack Mary's letter.

Perhaps the most iconic moment of an iconic reign was the defeat of the Spanish Armada. The *5.4 Match of the day: England versus Spain* lessons look at the motives for the Armada's launch and the ships of both navies, and contain a narrative cartoon that explains the reasons for the Armada's failure.

Lesson sequence

Lesson title	NC references	Objectives	Outcomes
5.1 Young Elizabeth: what was she like? pp72–73	The Elizabethan religious settlement and conflict with Catholics (including Scotland, Spain and Ireland)	• Investigate why Princess Elizabeth, King Henry VIII's youngest daughter, was such a clever student. • Examine the circumstances in which she became queen.	**All** students will describe Elizabeth's childhood. **Most** students will infer how different factors influenced Elizabeth. **Some** students will use empathetic understanding to explain how Elizabeth's family background influenced her.
5.2 What did Queen Elizabeth look like? pp74–75	The Elizabethan religious settlement and conflict with Catholics (including Scotland, Spain and Ireland)	• Explore why it is so hard to establish what Queen Elizabeth really looked like. • Examine why Elizabeth controlled her royal portraits so carefully. • Compare a number of royal portraits and judge which one would be most suitable for the queen.	**All** students will contrast sources about Elizabeth by identifying differences. **Most** students will compare and contrast interpretations of Elizabeth by cross-referencing sources. **Some** students will interpret symbolism in Elizabeth's portraits, making inferences by placing them in historical context.
5.3 Why did Queen Elizabeth kill her cousin? pp76–77	The Elizabethan religious settlement and conflict with Catholics (including Scotland, Spain and Ireland)	• Identify who Mary was and why she was heir to England's throne. • Examine the threat posed by Mary, Queen of Scots. • Investigate the Babington Plot.	**All** students will be able to identify reasons why Mary had to flee Scotland. **Most** students will describe the reasons for Mary's execution. **Some** students will explain the reasons for Mary's execution.
5.4A Match of the day: England versus Spain pp78–79 **5.4B Match of the day: England versus Spain** pp80–81	The Elizabethan religious settlement and conflict with Catholics (including Scotland, Spain and Ireland)	• Explore why the King of Spain decided to invade England in 1588. • Compare the strengths and weaknesses of England and Spain's navies. • Judge key reasons why the Spanish Armada failed.	**All** students will describe why relations between Spain and England were poor, and recall the events of the battle. **Most** students will explain why Philip wanted to attack Britain. **Some** students will analyse why Philip and the Spanish Armada failed.
Assessing Your Learning 2 pp82-83	The Elizabethan religious settlement and conflict with Catholics (including Scotland, Spain and Ireland)	• Identify and understand the symbolism of the Rainbow Portrait.	**All** students will identify several symbols and explain their meanings. **Most** students will select a variety of symbols and explain why Elizabeth would have been keen to display them. **Some** students will identify each symbol, relate it to Elizabeth and explain how portraits can be useful to historians.

Ideas for enrichment

Ask students to examine the Tudor family tree and chart Elizabeth's journey to the throne. Make sure the family tree is complete, and includes the branch that married into the Stuart family of Scotland. Pose the question: 'If Elizabeth were to die childless, who would take over?' You could extend this even further by asking students to chart our current monarch's family tree, posing the questions: 'Who will become monarch after Elizabeth II's death? And then who?' And so on!

Undertake a class research project that answers the question 'Why has Elizabeth's reign been called a "golden age"?' This could take the form of individual essays, or presentations, or perhaps a classroom display for lower ability students, who can each research a particular aspect of the 'golden age'.

Challenge students to find out about Britain's navy – The Royal Navy – today. How does it compare with Elizabeth's navy of 1588? Ask students to consider the size of the navy, its weaponry, and its roles.

The Hollywood blockbuster *Elizabeth: The Golden Age* (certificate 12A) gives a graphic account of the attempted invasion by the Spanish in 1588. You could watch clips (or the whole film as a treat) but why not challenge students to find out what is wrong with the film? Which parts are historically inaccurate? (Babington's assassination attempt, for example.) Which parts does it get right?

5.1 Young Elizabeth: what was she like?

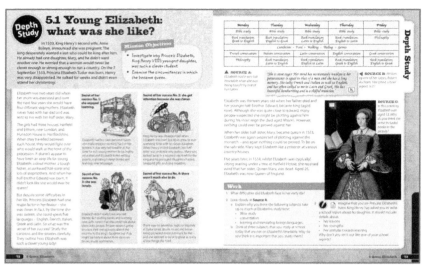

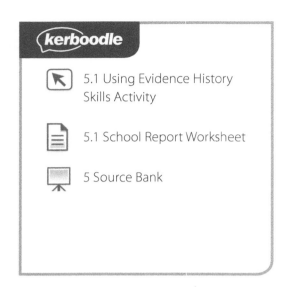

Renaissance, Revolution and Reformation pages 72–73

Lesson summary

Students will create a written report and/or piece of drama explaining how Elizabeth's childhood shaped the person she became. This lesson includes cross-curricular links to English (writing for a specific audience and purpose).

What are the lesson outcomes?

All students will describe Elizabeth's childhood.

Most students will infer how different factors influenced Elizabeth.

Some students will use empathetic understanding to explain how Elizabeth's family background influenced her.

Starter suggestion

- Students could create a small family tree showing the main members of the Tudor family. Following this, discussion could focus on what kind of a childhood Elizabeth might have had, based on her unusual family background!

Main learning suggestions and assessment

What activities will take place?

Task 1: Students should read pages 72–73 and use the information to complete Work activities **1–3**. They could complete 5.1 School Report Worksheet as an alternative to Work activity **3**. Otherwise, you could show them a traditional school report so they understand the format.

Task 2: Students should then imagine being Elizabeth's psychiatrist, or Head of Year at school, and write an email to a colleague about Elizabeth. This should include details about Elizabeth's special circumstances, for example, her problems in her home life and the effect it had on her.

Task 3: Students should create an episode of a soap opera called 'Tudor Turmoil' in which Elizabeth confronts her various family members about how they influenced her life.

Task 4: As an alternative to **Task 3**, students could create an article for a celebrity gossip magazine about Elizabeth's family life. In this article Elizabeth should be interviewed about how she feels about her childhood.

How will students demonstrate their understanding?

In **Task 1**, students will describe, explain and make inferences about Elizabeth's childhood. **Task 2** asks students to demonstrate these skills more explicitly. **Tasks 3** and **4** bring in the skill of empathetic understanding.

Plenary suggestions

- Students could complete 5.1 Using Evidence History Skills Activity. This task focuses on the skill of using a source as evidence and making inferences.

Differentiation suggestions

Support

- **Tasks 3** or **4** should be selected depending on the nature of the group. For some students extended writing may be more appropriate, while for others it may be more sensible for students to create their piece of drama without a script.

Extension: Hungry for more?

- Students could research the years that Elizabeth spent as her sister's prisoner. They could conduct a historical enquiry into this by formulating their own questions to frame their research, such as, 'Where was she imprisoned?' 'How did she spend her time?' 'How was she treated?'

5.2 What did Queen Elizabeth look like?

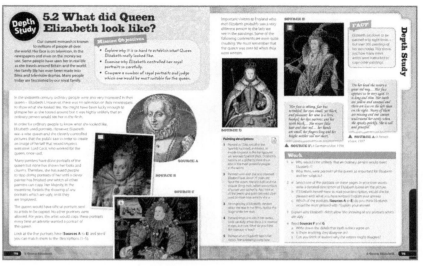

Renaissance, Revolution and Reformation pages 74–75

Lesson summary
Students will conduct a historical enquiry by annotating a range of sources with their different features. They will explain how Elizabeth used portraits as a form of propaganda by creating a 'perfect' portrait using symbolism. This lesson includes cross-curricular links to Art and English.

What are the lesson outcomes?
All students will contrast sources about Elizabeth by identifying differences.

Most students will compare and contrast interpretations of Elizabeth by cross-referencing sources.

Some students will interpret symbolism in Elizabeth's portraits, making inferences by placing them in historical context.

Starter suggestion
- Students could make a list of the ways in which they know about what our monarch or prime minister looks like. This could lead to a class discussion about why we need to know about our leaders.

Main learning suggestions and assessment
What activities will take place?
Task 1: Students should read pages 74–75 and use the information to complete Work activities **1–4** and 5.2 Paintings Worksheet 1.

Task 2: Set up five group tables and on each put a large copy of one of the **Sources A–E**. Each group should annotate the portrait on their table, using different colours from other groups. Give each group a different focus, such as: What does Elizabeth look like? What symbols can be

seen? What impression of Elizabeth do you get? Allow them two or three minutes to annotate a portrait, then they must move round to the next one. At the end, each group should feed back to the class about what they have learned about Elizabeth and how similar the sources are.

Task 3: Students should draw a self-portrait that includes five items to represent things that are important to them. This could then lead to a class discussion about how and why Elizabeth used symbolism within her portraits to influence what people thought of her.

Task 4: Students should then imagine being Elizabeth's court painter. They have to produce a 'perfect' portrait of Elizabeth, showing her in a light that she would approve of.

How will students demonstrate their understanding?
Task 1 encourages students to explore, compare and contrast sources. This skill is developed further in **Task 2**, where some students will interpret symbolism and make inferences using historical context. In **Task 3** students demonstrate their ability to use symbolism as an introduction to the skills needed in **Task 4**.

Plenary suggestions
- Students' work from **Task 4** could be displayed for the class to label the symbolism used, before giving a verdict on whether the painter would be 'employed' or 'eradicated!'

Differentiation suggestions
Support
- In **Task 2**, lower ability students could focus on what Elizabeth looks like and what they can see.

Extension: Hungry for more?
- Students could complete 5.2 Using Evidence History Skills Activity or 5.2 Paintings Worksheet 2, which focuses on the Armada Portrait.

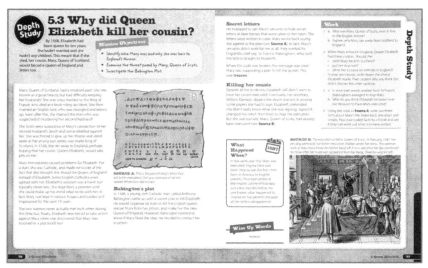

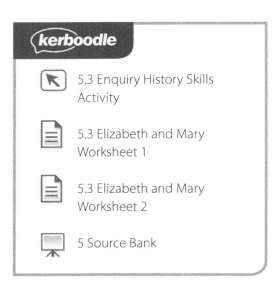

Renaissance, Revolution and Reformation pages 76–77

Lesson summary

Students will complete a series of activities that will help them to chart Mary's early life, her claim to the throne of England, and her execution. This lesson includes cross-curricular links to English (different styles of writing) and Citizenship (crime and punishment).

What are the lesson outcomes?

All students will be able to identify reasons why Mary had to flee Scotland.

Most students will describe the reasons for Mary's execution.

Some students will explain the reasons for Mary's execution.

Starter suggestion

- Students could be given a copy **Source A**, part of Mary's letter that led to her execution. They should use the decoder to work out what the letter says. Students could use 5.3 Elizabeth and Mary Worksheet 1 for this starter.

Main learning suggestions and assessment

What activities will take place?

Task 1: Students should read pages 76–77 and use the information to complete Work activities **1–4**.

Task 2: Students should make either a 'wanted' poster or a 'crimewatch' clip in which they describe the crimes Mary was suspected of committing in Scotland.

Task 3: Students should then be given an application form to complete for Mary, Queen of Scots, who is applying to be Queen of England. Why does she think she deserves the throne? Why does she think Elizabeth should not be queen? What qualities does she have that will make her a good queen? What experience does she have?

Task 4: Students should then create a 'death warrant' for Mary in which they explain the 'crimes' she has committed and the reasons why Elizabeth wants her dead!

How will students demonstrate their understanding?

In **Task 1**, students are able to identify, describe, and explain Mary's life from her escape from Scotland to her execution. In **Task 2**, they identify the events and actions that caused Mary to flee Scotland. **Task 3** requires students to select relevant evidence and information, and to demonstrate their ability to explain Mary's circumstances and make inferences about her character. In **Task 4** students will identify cause and consequence.

Plenary suggestions

- Students could write headlines for a newspaper article about Mary's execution, trying to sum up the reasons for her punishment or how they think Elizabeth might feel about it.

Differentiation suggestions

Support

- In **Task 2**, there are two different activities to choose from, depending on students' abilities.

Extension: Hungry for more?

- Students could complete 5.3 Elizabeth and Mary Worksheet 2, which asks students to write a diary entry as Elizabeth when she has learned of Mary's betrayal.

- Students could also complete 5.3 Enquiry History Skills Activity. This activity guides students through the process of creating their own enquiry question about Mary.

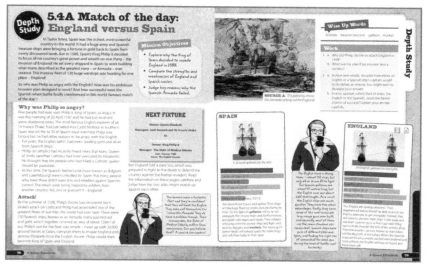

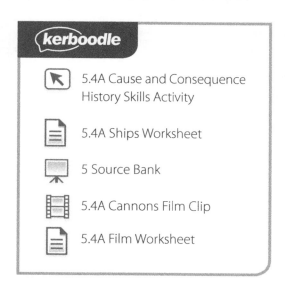

Renaissance, Revolution and Reformation pages 78–79

Lesson summary

Students will create a football-style commentary explaining why Philip wanted to attack England. They will also decide which fleet was strongest. This lesson includes a focus on literacy (writing styles, speaking and listening) and numeracy (bar and line graphs).

What are the lesson outcomes?

All students will describe why relations between Spain and England were poor, and recall the events of the battle.

Most students will explain why Philip wanted to attack Britain.

Some students will analyse why Philip and the Spanish Armada failed.

Starter suggestion

- Students could be shown **Source A**, a painting of the Spanish Armada, and asked to choose five words to describe the fleet.

Main learning suggestions and assessment

What activities will take place?

Task 1: Students should read pages 78–79 and use the information to complete Work activities **1–2**. Students could also create a comparative graph for Work activity **2b**. They should use the details on page 79 to plot the ratings for each category for the two galleons on either a bar chart or a line graph.

Task 2: Students should watch 5.4A Cannons Film Clip and then complete 5.4A Film Worksheet. They should also complete 5.4A Cause and Consequence History Skills Activity to check their understanding.

Task 3: Students should use the information in the *Student Book* to write their own football-style commentary about the lead up to the Spanish Armada. They should include: pre-match interviews in which the 'star players' (Drake, Elizabeth, and Philip) talk about the grudge between the two countries; Drake's attack on Cadiz; a 'half time' interview with representatives from Spain and England about their tactics and plans; and a match analysis of what they think the outcome will be.

How will students demonstrate their understanding?

Tasks 1 and **3** allow students to describe, explain, and analyse events. **Task 3** supports comparing and contrasting skills.

Plenary suggestions

- In one of the tasks in the next lesson, students are asked to consider cause and consequence. As a bridge to this, students could make a list of the strengths and weaknesses of each side at this stage of the 'match'.

Differentiation suggestions

Support

- In **Task 3**, students could use a writing frame in which the main commentator asks questions and the people who should answer are identified.

Extension: Hungry for more?

- Students should complete 5.4A Ships Worksheet and use their answers to help them create an advert for either a Spanish or an English galleon. Their advert should include information on why this galleon is better than the competition's galleon.

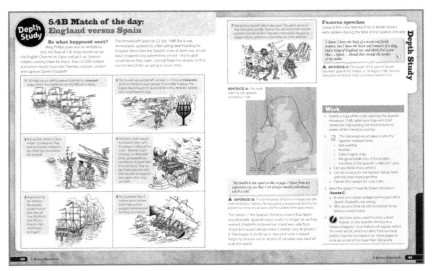

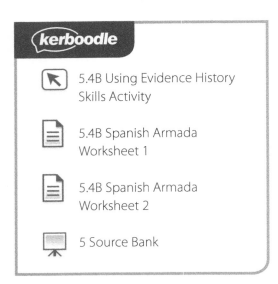

Renaissance, Revolution and Reformation pages 80–81

Lesson summary

Students will categorize causes of the defeat of the Spanish Armada into a table. They will also analyse and evaluate the most important reasons for the English victory. This lesson includes cross-curricular links to English (essay writing).

What are the lesson outcomes?

All students will describe why relations between Spain and England were poor, and recall the events of the battle.

Most students will explain why Philip wanted to attack Britain.

Some students will analyse why Philip and the Spanish Armada failed.

Starter suggestion

- Students could be asked to consolidate their knowledge from the previous lesson by completing 'speech bubbles' for Philip, Elizabeth, Drake, and the Duke of Medina Sidonia about their thoughts during the build-up to the Spanish Armada.

Main learning suggestions and assessment

What activities will take place?

Task 1: Students should read pages 80–81 and use the information to complete Work activities **1–4**.

Task 2: Students should complete a table in which they categorize information about why the Spanish lost into three groups: The English were well organized; The Spanish were not well organized; Chance/luck. 5.4B Spanish Armada Worksheet 1 provides an alternate approach to this activity.

Task 3: Students should use the ideas they formulated in **Task 2** to write an essay entitled: 'Why did England beat the Spanish Armada?'

Task 4: Students should use 5.4B Spanish Armada Worksheet 2 to design a medal to celebrate the English victory over the Spanish.

How will students demonstrate their understanding?

In **Task 2**, students refine their ability to identify and explain reasons for the Spanish defeat, and analyse the relationships between these reasons. In **Task 3** they explain, analyse, and evaluate the factors that led the English to victory. **Task 3** can be used as formative assessment.

Plenary suggestions

- Students could be asked to link this lesson to their prior knowledge about the development of the British Empire and explorers, to explain the greater significance of the English victory. To scaffold this discussion, small groups could be asked to discuss the question, 'Why was the defeat of the Spanish Armada a significant event in English history?' They could then feed back their ideas to the rest of the class.

Differentiation suggestions

Support

- In **Task 2**, students could be given varying numbers of cards to categorize, depending on their ability.

- In Work activity **4**, you could show students examples of history magazines or journals so they can understand the genre they are to write in.

Extension: Hungry for more?

- In 5.4B Using Evidence History Skills Activity, students consider the speech given by Elizabeth to the men facing the Spanish Armada. Students could work out what she is saying and explain why they think it has become such a famous speech.

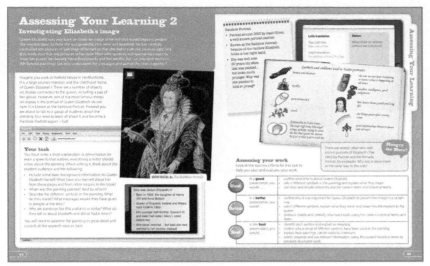

Renaissance, Revolution and Reformation pages 82–83

Assessment in the *Student Book*

In this assessment task, students are asked to analyse symbolism within a visual source, using their contextual knowledge to explain how Elizabeth used portraits as propaganda to convey certain messages to her people. They create a short explanation or presentation that outlines everything a visitor to Hatfield House in Hertfordshire should know about the Rainbow Portrait of Elizabeth.

This assessment allows students to develop their ability to conduct historical enquiries; to consider the significance of the actions of key individuals; and to use and critically evaluate sources.

In the *Student Book* (and on the supporting worksheets) you will find guidance of success criteria that you can use to help your students understand what their work should include. You could ask them to use these criteria for self- or peer-assessment once they have completed the task.

Chapter 5 Queen Elizabeth assessment task

You must produce a short written explanation, presentation or speech that outlines everything a visitor should know about the Rainbow Portrait. When writing it, think about the following:

- Include some basic background on Queen Elizabeth herself. What have you learned about her from the *Student Book*?

- When was the painting painted? And by whom?

- Describe the different symbols in the painting.

- Try to explain why paintings like this are useful to us today. What do they tell us about Elizabeth and about Tudor times?

Student Book
- Assessment task
- Student 'Assessing your work' grid

kerboodle
- Assessment Task Presentation 2
- Assessment Worksheet 2
- Success Criteria Teacher Grid 2

Teacher Handbook
- Success Criteria Teacher Grid 2

Hungry for More?

There are several other very well-known portraits of Elizabeth (the Ditchley Portrait and the Armada Portrait, for example). Why not analyse them in the same way as this one?

Assessing your work

In a **good** presentation, you would…	<ul><li>outline several facts about Queen Elizabeth</li><li>select different symbols in the painting and explain what they mean</li><li>use clear and simple sentences and the correct dates and historical terms.</li></ul>
In a **better** presentation, you would…	<ul><li>outline why it was important for Queen Elizabeth to present her image in a certain way</li><li>select different symbols, explain what they mean, and relate this to the queen</li><li>create a clearly and carefully structured piece of work, using the correct historical terms and dates.</li></ul>
In the **best** presentation, you would…	<ul><li>identify each symbol and explain its meaning</li><li>outline why a range of different symbols have been used in the painting</li><li>explain how paintings can be useful to historians</li><li>select, organize and use relevant information, using the correct historical terms to produce structured work.</li></ul>

Tip

Since this task relies heavily on visual imagery, it might work well with annotated illustrations, possibly in the form of a PowerPoint or movie, or a written presentation with visual images included in the text. All images examined in this assessment are available on 5 Source Bank on Kerboodle.

Success criteria teacher grid

Assessment criteria	Beginning/ Developing	Securing	Extending
	Current NC Level 3/4	Current NC Level 5/6	Current NC Level 7/8
	GCSE Grade Indicator E/D	GCSE Grade Indicator C/B	GCSE Grade Indicator A/A*
Remembering	Student can list three facts about Elizabeth I	Student can describe in detail key events from Elizabeth I's reign	
Understanding	Student can explain how the Rainbow Portrait got its name	Student can provide a basic history of the Rainbow Portrait including when it was painted and by whom	Student can explain any reasons why Elizabeth may have chosen to have the Rainbow Portrait created
Applying	Student can select different symbols in the painting and explain what they mean	Student can select different symbols, explain what they mean, and relate this to the queen	Student can outline why Elizabeth used a range of different symbols in the painting
Analyzing	Student can identify how they think Elizabeth wanted to be portrayed in this image	Student can outline why it was important for Queen Elizabeth to present her image in a certain way	Student can assess how Elizabeth chose to be portrayed in the Rainbow Portrait and why this might have been
Evaluating	Student can identify reasons why monarchs chose to have their portrait painted	Student can explain how paintings can be useful to historians	Student should judge how useful the Rainbow Portrait is to historians studying Elizabeth I
Creating	Student attempts to use the correct historical terminology and their response is structured appropriately	Student can select, organize and use relevant information, including the correct historical terms, to produce a well-structured piece of work	Student can select, organize and research a wide range of relevant information and use the correct historical terms to produce a well-structured piece of work

Overview:
Chapter 6 Exit the Tudors, enter the Stuarts

Helping you deliver KS3 History National Curriculum

This chapter introduces students to another of Britain's most famous ruling dynasties and introduces the idea of a united kingdom. There are a number of key historical terms highlighted in the chapter, such as the 'Divine Right of Kings', that are essential for students to learn.

There are some wonderful sources for students to analyse, and a source-based enquiry encourages students to question accepted versions of events and make judgements based on evidence. By the end of the chapter students will also have had the opportunity to analyse causes and consequences of events, argue for and/ or against a particular point of view, use key historical terminology appropriately, and increase their knowledge and understanding of key historical events.

The Big Picture

Why are we teaching 'Exit the Tudors, enter the Stuarts'?

The Tudor dynasty casts such a long shadow over this period that it is easy for some students to overlook the Stuarts. For this reason we have explicitly highlighted the changeover from one royal house to another, and decided to dedicate this chapter to some of the significant events that occurred during the reign of King James I of England and VI of Scotland.

The chapter begins with the death of Queen Elizabeth and the accession of her closest living relative as the monarch of both England and Scotland. The chapter then moves on to look at the famous Gunpowder Plot. If there is one historical event that all children have some background knowledge of, it is this. In our experience, however, this background knowledge can be wildly inaccurate! After the lesson that

Skills and processes covered in this chapter

		6.1	6.2	6.3	6.4	6.5A	6.5B
History skills	Historical enquiry			✓		✓	✓
	Using evidence and source work	✓	✓	✓	✓		✓
	Chronological understanding			✓		✓	
	Understanding cultural, ethnic and religious diversity	✓	✓	✓	✓	✓	✓
	Change and continuity	✓			✓	✓	
	Cause and consequence	✓	✓	✓	✓	✓	✓
	Significance					✓	
	Interpretations	✓		✓			
	Making links/connections	✓	✓	✓		✓	✓
	Explores similarities and differences				✓		
Literacy and numeracy	Key words identified/deployed	✓			✓		✓
	Extended writing	✓	✓	✓			✓
	Encourages reading for meaning	✓	✓	✓	✓	✓	✓
	Focuses on structuring writing		✓				
	Asks students to use writing to explore and develop ideas	✓	✓	✓	✓		✓
	Learn through talk/discussion		✓	✓			✓
	Numeracy opportunities						
Activity types	Creative task	✓	✓		✓		✓
	Emphasizes role of individual		✓	✓			
	Group work						
	Independent research						
	Develops study skills	✓		✓			✓

sets out the accepted version of events, the 'History Mystery' lesson asks students to consider an alternative version of events and to decide whether Guy Fawkes and the rest of the plotters were the victims of a seventeenth-century conspiracy. Questioning an event really fires students' imaginations and can often get them to question the accuracy of others – the mark of a real historian!

The fact that witchery was the cause of such hysteria during James' reign amuses the students no end – as do the case studies of people who were convicted of and executed for witchcraft. This topic also provides a wonderful example of the conclusions people leaped to under the influence of fear and in the absence of rational explanation.

Arguably, the most significant event of James' reign was the journey of the pilgrims to North America. We tell their incredible story through a fun and engaging narrative. The fact that Americans speak English and that they have a city named New York is something that many students have never questioned. Teaching this lesson can often lead to 'eureka' moments when you can actually see the long-term repercussions of the *Mayflower*'s voyage dawn on students.

Lesson sequence

Lesson title	NC references	Objectives	Outcomes
6.1 The scruffy Stuart! pp84–85	The Elizabethan religious settlement and conflict with Catholics (including Scotland, Spain and Ireland)	• Explain why the throne of England passed to the Scottish royal family. • Discover what England's new Scottish king believed about his 'Divine Right'.	**All** students will identify features of a visual source. **Most** students will use evidence from a source to make inferences about how successful James I was as king. **Some** students will analyse how useful a source is, and consider its value and limitations.
6.2 Remember, remember the fifth of November! pp86–87	The Elizabethan religious settlement and conflict with Catholics (including Scotland, Spain and Ireland)	• Recall at least five accepted facts about the Gunpowder Plot. • Identify the role of key individuals in the story of the Gunpowder Plot.	**All** students will identify key individuals involved in the Gunpowder Plot. **Most** students will describe the Gunpowder Plot. **Some** students will explain their initial thoughts about whether or not Guy Fawkes and his co-conspirators were treated fairly.
6.3 History Mystery: Were the gunpowder plotters framed? pp88–89	The Elizabethan religious settlement and conflict with Catholics (including Scotland, Spain and Ireland)	• Evaluate evidence like a 'history mystery' detective. • Decide whether you think the gunpowder plotters were framed or not.	**All** students will match evidence to statements that suggest that the plotters were framed. **Most** students will explain pieces of evidence by making inferences from them. **Some** students will analyse the Gunpowder Plot in order to evaluate whether or not the plotters were framed.
6.4 Which witch is which? pp90–91	Society, economy and culture across the period	• Explore why witchcraft was so widely believed in. • Identify the type of people accused of witchcraft. • Analyse sources from Stuart times.	**All** students will recall facts about the 'witch craze' of the Tudor and Stuart eras. **Most** students will explain what type of person was most likely to be accused of witchcraft. **Some** students will explain why people in this era believed in witchcraft.
6.5A Why do Americans speak English? pp92–93 **6.5B Why do Americans speak English?** pp94–95	The first colony in America and first contact with India	• Discover why and how the English began to settle in North America. • Explain why most Americans speak English.	**All** students will describe early settlement in North America. **Most** students will use empathy to explain what life was like for the pilgrims. **Some** students will explain why English colonies came to dominate North America.

Ideas for enrichment

Why not investigate the origins behind some place names in North America? This can start on the east coast with places like New York, New Jersey, New Hampshire, New England, and Nova Scotia, before moving onto Louisiana, New Orleans, and South Carolina. Then look at names in western parts of North America such as San Diego, San Francisco, and Los Angeles.

The Union Flag provides a great extension opportunity. Ask students to hold their own competition to design a flag to celebrate the union between England and Scotland.

Students could write and perform a play entitled 'The Gunpowder Plot' – they can choose the accepted version of events, or the one involving Robert Cecil.

How about setting students the task of naming our current era? They know about the Tudor and Stuart periods – will they name our current era after the royal family, or some other aspect of life?

6.1 The scruffy Stuart!

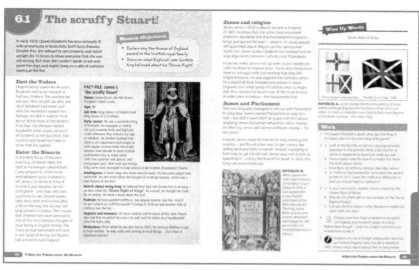

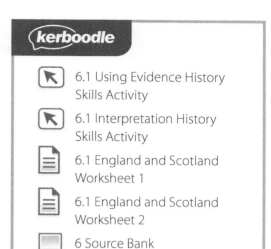

Renaissance, Revolution and Reformation pages 84–85

Lesson summary

Students will complete a 'layers of inference' activity in order to decide how useful a source is to a historian studying the reign of James I.

What are the lesson outcomes?

All students will identify features of a visual source.

Most students will use evidence from a source to make inferences about how successful James I was as king.

Some students will analyse how useful a source is, and consider its value and limitations.

Starter suggestion

- Give students a copy of the portrait of James I on page 84 of the *Student Book*. Ask them to annotate it with words to describe the impression it gives them.

Main learning suggestions and assessment

What activities will take place?

Task 1: Students should read pages 84–85 and use the information to complete Work activities **1–5**.

Task 2: Students should consider how useful **Source B** is to a historian studying how successful James I was as king. They could complete a 'layers of inference' activity:

What can you see in the source?
Using your own knowledge, what can you infer about King James I using this source?
What limitations does the source have?

Students should be given the following checklist before having a go at their own answer:

	Briefly describe the source.
	Identify whether the source tells us about James' successes or weaknesses as king.
	Use your own knowledge to explain this aspect of James' reign.
	Use your own knowledge to explain a limitation of the source: what do you know about James I that a historian couldn't find out about from this source?

Task 3: Students should then use the checklist to peer-assess each other's work, offering ideas for improvement. Each pair of students could then team up to write a 'perfect' answer.

How will students demonstrate their understanding?

Students will learn how to analyse the usefulness of a source.

Plenary suggestions

- Students could complete 6.1 Interpretations History Skills Activity, which encourages them to reflect on the different ways in which James is viewed.

Differentiation suggestions

Support

- In **Task 2** lower ability students could be directed to play 'I spy' in the first layer; identify what the source is about in the second layer; and decide if this shows James I in a positive or negative light in the final layer.

Extension: Hungry for more?

- Students could complete either 6.1 England and Scotland Worksheet 1 or Worksheet 2, both of which would work well as homework.

- Students could also complete 6.1 Using Evidence History Skills Activity.

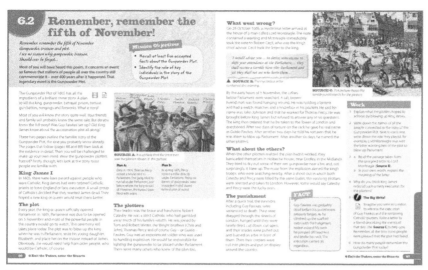

Renaissance, Revolution and Reformation pages 86–87

Lesson summary

Students will create a social networking profile for Guy Fawkes, in order to describe the Gunpowder Plot. This lesson includes cross-curricular links to English (writing in an informal manner).

What are the lesson outcomes?

All students will identify key individuals involved in the Gunpowder Plot.

Most students will describe the Gunpowder Plot.

Some students will explain their initial thoughts about whether or not Guy Fawkes and his co-conspirators were treated fairly.

Starter suggestion

- Students could be shown the poem 'Remember, remember the fifth of November' and asked to illustrate it, showing the historical events that inspired it, or to write a paragraph explaining what it is about. This allows you to check prior knowledge.

Main learning suggestions and assessment

What activities will take place?

Task 1: Students should read pages 86–87 and use the information to complete Work activities **1–6**.

Task 2: Students should create a social networking profile for Guy Fawkes (or one of the other conspirators), which includes: his religion; his nationality; his friends; conversations between the plotters; a portrait as his profile picture.

Task 3: Students should watch 6.2 Mystery Film Clip and complete 6.2 Film Worksheet.

Task 4: In the next lesson students will complete a 'history mystery' in which they work out whether the plotters were

framed or not. As an introduction to this, students could identify any information that they feel could show that Guy Fawkes' trial was not fully fair.

How will students demonstrate their understanding?

This lesson is vitally important for ensuring that students have contextual knowledge about the Gunpowder Plot, prior to completing *6.3 History Mystery: Were the gunpowder plotters framed?* In **Tasks 1–3** students are able to identify, describe, and explain events and ideas.

Plenary suggestions

- Students could be asked to act as Guy Fawkes' defence lawyer and write a short introductory statement to give when the court case opens.

- Students could complete 6.2 Using Evidence History Skills Activity after watching 6.2 Execution Mini-Movie.

Differentiation suggestions

Support

- In **Task 2**, lower ability students could be given a social networking profile template that contains the categories of information they need to include and a couple of 'posts' from other conspirators to prompt a discussion about the plot.

- For Work activity **5**, you might like to remind students of the conventions of a letter, such as including addresses and the date.

Extension: Hungry for more?

- Students could create a spread for a children's book. One side should describe how we traditionally remember the Gunpowder Plot on bonfire night, and the other side should explain the historical reasons for these traditions.

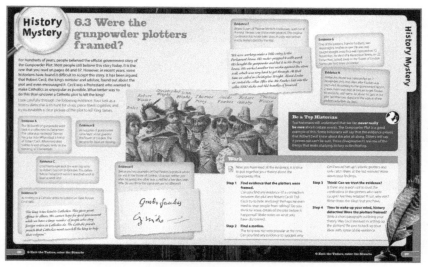

Renaissance, Revolution and Reformation pages 88–89

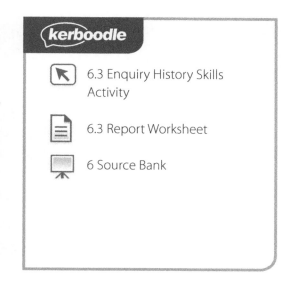

Lesson summary

Students will conduct an investigation into whether they think the gunpowder plotters were framed, and will then campaign for their freedom.

What are the lesson outcomes?

All students will match evidence to statements that suggest that the plotters were framed.

Most students will explain pieces of evidence by making inferences from them.

Some students will analyse the Gunpowder Plot in order to evaluate whether or not the plotters were framed.

Starter suggestion

- Students' knowledge from the previous lesson could be consolidated by asking them to summarize the story of the Gunpowder Plot in five sentences.

Main learning suggestions and assessment

What activities will take place?

Task 1: Students should read pages 88–89 and use the information to complete the Work activity. This activity leads students through a step-by-step investigation of the evidence and 6.3 Enquiry History Skills Activity supports analysing the evidence as a whole-class activity. The full evidence paraphrased in this activity is available in the *Student Book*.

Task 2: Students could then work in pairs or small groups to plan and present a 'Free Guido' campaign. They should protest that the plotters were innocent and use evidence from their investigation to support their ideas.

Task 3: Students should create a television news report about the death of the plotters, including interviews with people who believe that the plotters were framed. They

should ask Robert Cecil some questions that try to get to the bottom of this accusation!

How will students demonstrate their understanding?

In **Task 1**, students follow the steps to work out: what can be inferred from each source; why the king might want to frame the plotters; how reliable the evidence is; whether the plotters were framed. This process allows students to demonstrate their ability to describe, explain, analyse, and evaluate evidence.

Plenary suggestions

- Students could 'vote with their feet'. Ask them to move to one side of the classroom or the other, in order to show whether or not they agree with the interpretation that the gunpowder plotters were framed, and then to verbally explain their ideas.

Differentiation suggestions

Support

- In **Task 1**, students could be given a list of statements such as: 'There was no way the plotters could get hold of gunpowder'. They need to match a piece of evidence to each statement. To make this activity kinaesthetic, students could be given copies of each piece of evidence that they could match to each statement.

- 6.3 Report Worksheet provides a framework for the written task in the *Student Book*.

Extension: Hungry for more?

- Students could create a 'wanted' poster for either Guido Fawkes or Robert Cecil, depending on whether or not they agree that the plotters were framed. Their posters should explain what 'crime' the suspect has committed.

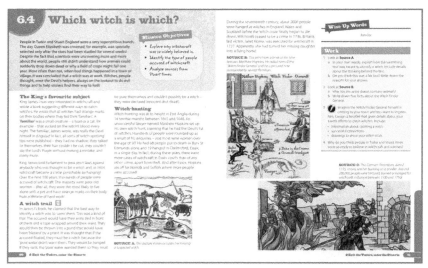

Renaissance, Revolution and Reformation pages 90–91

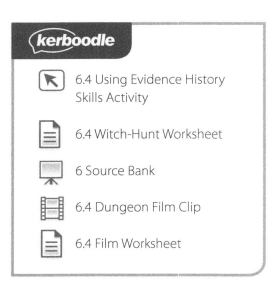

Lesson summary

Students will decide who was most likely to be accused of witchcraft, using criteria they have compiled themselves. This lesson could include cross-curricular links to PSHE, with class discussions focusing on persecution and peer pressure.

What are the lesson outcomes?

All students will recall facts about the 'witch craze' of the Tudor and Stuart eras.

Most students will explain what type of person was most likely to be accused of witchcraft.

Some students will explain why people in this era believed in witchcraft.

Starter suggestion

- Students could be given a copy of **Source A**, on page 90, and a list of captions to annotate it with. They could then suggest a hypothesis about what is going on.

Main learning suggestions and assessment

What activities will take place?

Task 1: Students should read pages 90–91 and use the information to complete Work activities **1–4** and either 6.4 Using Evidence History Skills Activity or 6.4 Witch-Hunt Worksheet.

Task 2: Students should create a list of things to watch out for when trying to spot a witch. Members of the class should be given descriptions of fictional characters and called to the front to be 'interviewed' by Matthew Hopkins (you, the teacher). The class could then use their list of criteria to work out which characters could be accused of witchcraft.

Task 3: Students should then pretend that they are Matthew Hopkins and have to complete a form to claim payment for

finding a 'witch'. How can he prove that the suspect is guilty of witchcraft?

Task 4: Students should watch 6.4 Dungeon Film Clip and complete 6.4 Film Worksheet.

How will students demonstrate their understanding?

In **Task 1**, Work activities **1**, **2** and **3** support students in selecting and recalling relevant information, while Work activity **4** (and the plenary activity) gives students the opportunity to explain why they think belief in witchcraft was so widespread. **Tasks 2** and **3** allow students to demonstrate their ability to explain how 'witches' were identified.

Plenary suggestions

- Start a discussion about why some people were more vulnerable to being accused of witchcraft. Following this, students could be asked to think of contemporary parallels in which vulnerable people are treated differently because they are different, or where peer pressure leads to people allowing the victimisation of others.

Differentiation suggestions

Support

- In **Task 2**, students could be given a list of things to look for when trying to spot a witch, or a checklist to complete to focus their ideas:

	Female?	Old?	Pets/ familiars?	Devil marks?	Lives alone?
Suspect 1:					

Extension: Hungry for more?

- Students could find out what was ironic about Matthew Hopkins' death, or they could investigate when the last person was tried for witchcraft in Britain.

6.5A Why do Americans speak English?

Renaissance, Revolution and Reformation pages 92–93

Lesson summary
Students will create a piece of writing and a piece of drama to illustrate what life was like for the pilgrims when they arrived in America. This lesson includes cross-curricular links to English and Drama.

What are the lesson outcomes?
All students will describe early settlement in North America.

Most students will use empathy to explain what life was like for the pilgrims.

Some students will explain why English colonies came to dominate North America.

Starter suggestion
- Students could be asked what kind of words and qualities come to mind when they hear the word 'pilgrim'.

Main learning suggestions and assessment
What activities will take place?
Task 1: Students should read the cartoon on pages 92–93 and then complete 6.5A Puritans Worksheet, which asks them to consider the problems the early settlers faced.

Task 2: Students should write a 'postcard' from one of the pilgrims to their family in England, describing their experiences.

Task 3: Students should decorate the front of their 'postcard' with a picture that summarizes the experiences of the pilgrims.

Task 4: Students should then create a piece of drama in which they present a television show featuring people from the 1620s deciding whether to move abroad and settle in North America. The show should feature a presenter who is trying to persuade people to go, and a family of settlers.

How will students demonstrate their understanding?
In **Tasks 2** and **3**, students will demonstrate empathetic understanding by describing and explaining how different situations and events affected the pilgrims.

Plenary suggestions
- Students could create a round for a class quiz. Each team should come up with two questions (with answers) about early settlers in North America. Following this, students could take part in a class quiz to see who has learned the most this lesson!

- Students could complete 6.5A Significance History Skills Activity on Walter Raleigh.

Differentiation suggestions
Support
- Lower ability students could be given a list of words to include in **Task 2**, or a writing frame complete with sentence starters.

- In **Task 4** students could be grouped to ensure that differentiation through peer support is available. Alternatively, they could be provided with a partially complete script, which includes questions for the presenter to ask the family of settlers.

Extension: Hungry for more?
- Students could research the American holiday of Thanksgiving and what it celebrates. They could then use this information to create either a children's story book or Thanksgiving cards, explaining the real meaning of the holiday.

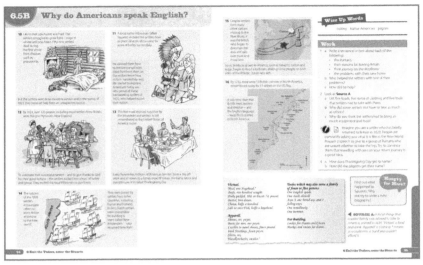

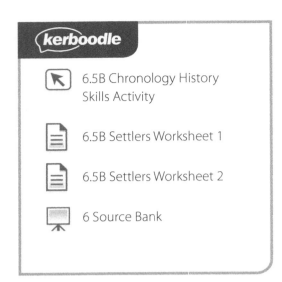

Renaissance, Revolution and Reformation pages 94–95

Lesson summary
Students will create a piece of writing and a piece of drama to illustrate what life was like for the pilgrims when they arrived in America. This lesson includes cross-curricular links to English and Drama.

What are the lesson outcomes?
All students will describe early settlement in North America.

Most students will use empathy to explain what life was like for the Pilgrim Fathers.

Some students will explain why English colonies came to dominate Northern America.

Starter suggestion
- Students could select items for a pilgrim to pack before setting off for the New World. They could either draw items into a picture of an empty suitcase, or select from a pile of actual items. Students could then choose their most vital item and explain why it should be included.

Main learning suggestions and assessment
What activities will take place?
Task 1: Students should read pages 94–95 and use the information to complete Work activities **1–4**. They should also complete 6.5B Chronology History Skills Activity to check their understanding of America's colonization by England. 6.5B Settlers Worksheet 2 provides a framework for Work activity 3, where students must write a letter to a group of Puritans to encourage them to move to the New World.

Task 2: Students should be asked to assume the role of a museum curator who is developing an exhibition on the first English colonies in America. They need to decide which artefacts to display, and how to inform visitors about the exhibits.

Task 3: Students should create an audio guide for their exhibition explaining the plight of early settlers in North America and explaining why it is that English is still spoken in the USA today.

Task 4: Students should write a letter to schoolteachers, telling them about their exhibition and why a school trip to the museum could help students' understanding of this topic.

How will students demonstrate their understanding?
In **Task 2** students' exhibitions should be given the title 'Why do Americans speak English?' This will help students to focus their ideas and demonstrate their ability to analyse why it was English settlers, rather than people from other countries, that came to dominate North America.

Plenary suggestions
- A class discussion, focusing on the key question, 'Why do Americans speak English?' could be used to summarize ideas and check students' understanding.

Differentiation suggestions
Support
- In **Task 2** organize students into groups where they will either support or stretch each other. Each member of the group could be given a role, such as 'director', 'researcher', or 'artist'.

Extension: Hungry for more?
- Students could consider how accurate historical interpretations of early settlers in North America and the Native Americans are by watching a film such as Disney's *Pocahontas.*

Overview:
Chapter 7 England at war

Helping you deliver KS3 History National Curriculum

The events covered in this chapter were crucial in establishing the type of government we have today, and are mentioned in the KS3 History National Curriculum for 2014.

Establishing cause and consequence – a key History skill – will be addressed. By the end of the chapter, students should certainly be aware that most events have a number of causes (both short- and long-term), and that consequences can also be of different kinds (such as short- and long-term). Throughout the chapter students will be challenged to select and combine information from sources to answer questions, evaluate the strengths and weaknesses of those sources, and assess the significance of events, individuals, ideas and beliefs.

The Big Picture

Why are we teaching 'England at war'?

The causes, major events, and dramatic consequences of the English Civil War have been addressed throughout this chapter. The main issues that tore the nation apart in the mid-seventeenth century are investigated through a series of 'talking heads'. These clearly establish the grievances felt by both sides before the outbreak of hostilities. We then examine how the war was fought, considering the weapons and tactics used, in a 'match of the day' style.

The next lessons reinforce the distinctions between the two sides, requiring students to consider the problems that come with leadership. The importance of discipline in a fighting force is also highlighted. We look at the setup of Cromwell's army while simultaneously informing the students of the religious background and motivation of Cromwell and his men.

Skills and processes covered in this chapter

		7.1	7.2	7.3	7.4	7.5A	7.5B	7.6
History skills	Historical enquiry	✓				✓	✓	
	Using evidence and source work			✓	✓	✓	✓	✓
	Chronological understanding					✓	✓	
	Understanding cultural, ethnic and religious diversity	✓	✓	✓	✓			
	Change and continuity				✓			✓
	Cause and consequence	✓			✓	✓	✓	✓
	Significance				✓	✓	✓	✓
	Interpretations			✓				
	Making links/connections					✓	✓	
	Explores similarities and differences	✓						✓
Literacy and numeracy	Key words identified/deployed	✓	✓	✓			✓	✓
	Extended writing					✓	✓	✓
	Encourages reading for meaning		✓	✓	✓	✓	✓	✓
	Focuses on structuring writing				✓			✓
	Asks students to use writing to explore and develop ideas	✓		✓	✓	✓	✓	✓
	Learn through talk/discussion					✓	✓	✓
	Numeracy opportunities						✓	
Activity types	Creative task		✓	✓	✓	✓	✓	✓
	Emphasizes role of individual	✓		✓	✓	✓	✓	
	Group work					✓		
	Independent research		✓				✓	
	Develops study skills			✓	✓		✓	✓

The immediate consequence of the Royalist defeat is played out in a courtroom drama between Charles I and Judge Bradshaw. This is a source-based exercise, which allows the students to piece together the dramatic details for themselves, while 'stop and think' bubbles prompt them to consider some pertinent points. We have presented Charles' punishment in the sensationalist way that modern television might, in order to convey both the shock and spectacular nature of the event.

Lesson sequence

Lesson title	NC references	Objectives	Outcomes
7.1 Why did the English start fighting each other? pp96–97	The causes and events of the civil wars throughout Britain	• Examine why King Charles I, son of James I, had become so unpopular. • Compare the two sides fighting the English Civil War. • Define the term 'civil war'.	**All** students will answer questions about, and write an essay describing, the causes of the Civil War. **Most** students will write an essay explaining why the Civil War was caused by the king and/or Parliament. **Some** students will categorize and analyse the causes of the Civil War.
7.2 Match of the day: Roundheads versus Cavaliers pp98–99	The causes and events of the civil wars throughout Britain	• Examine which sections of society supported each side in the Civil War. • Summarize how soldiers fought in the Civil War and outline what they looked like.	**All** students will select and categorize information about the Civil War. **Most** students will use evidence to explain the strengths and/or weaknesses of each side in the Civil War. **Some** students will use evidence and critical thinking skills to decide which side was most likely to win the Civil War.
7.3 Prince Rupert: mad Cavalier or sad Cavalier? pp100–101	The causes and events of the civil wars throughout Britain	• Recall who Prince Rupert was and why he was so popular with the king's supporters. • Discover what the Roundheads thought of him and how they tried to damage his reputation. • Define the word 'propaganda'.	**All** students will identify the meaning of two sources about Prince Rupert. **Most** students will use evidence from the sources to explain their meaning and purpose. **Some** students will use evidence from the sources and their contextual knowledge in order to explain the meaning and purpose of the sources.
7.4 What was new about the New Model Army? pp102–103	The causes and events of the civil wars throughout Britain	• Summarize why Parliament needed to improve its army. • Recall who was responsible for the training of Parliament's New Model Army. • Examine how their strict discipline made them a more effective fighting force.	**All** students will identify why the historian Peter Moss thinks the New Model Army was so successful. **Most** students will use contextual knowledge to explain a historical interpretation. **Some** students will explain why Moss has made these conclusions, using what they know about contemporary beliefs and situations to put his interpretation in context.
7.5A Why was King Charles I sentenced to death? pp104–105 **7.5B Why was King Charles I sentenced to death? pp106–107**	The causes and events of the civil wars throughout Britain	• Explore how and why King Charles was put on trial. • Analyse the key events of the trial. • Investigate how the judges arrived at their verdict.	**All** students will use empathy and bias to create an account of Charles' trial, from the perspective of a Royalist or a Parliamentarian. **Most** students will use contextual knowledge and a variety of sources to explain why Charles believed Parliament could not try him. **Some** students will use and analyse sources, testing their reliability and making inferences from them, in order to decide whether or not it was inevitable that Charles was found guilty.
7.6 Charlie for the chop! pp108–109	The causes and events of the civil wars throughout Britain	• Explore how Charles spent the last few hours of his life. • Examine the details of his execution. • Evaluate sources relating to the execution.	**All** students will select and summarize information about Charles I in order to write an obituary. **Most** students will use their prior knowledge to describe the life and death of Charles I. **Some** students will use their prior knowledge and a critical analysis of a range of sources to explain different aspects and interpretations of the life and death of Charles I.

Ideas for enrichment

The English Civil War Society can be contacted at www.english-civil-war-society.org.uk and are more than willing to organize a demonstration of period weapons and stage mock battles. It makes for a memorable day and certainly puts the History department on the map for staff and students alike.

Ask students to research and present a display about Britain at war today. Alternatively, split the class into groups and set them the challenge of writing and performing their own play entitled 'King Charles' last day'. They love doing this!

I have been lucky enough to find the TV series *Children of the New Forest* on DVD. It follows the trials and tribulations of the Beverleys, a Royalist family, during the latter part of the Civil War. It is brilliant, and a great reward for your students!

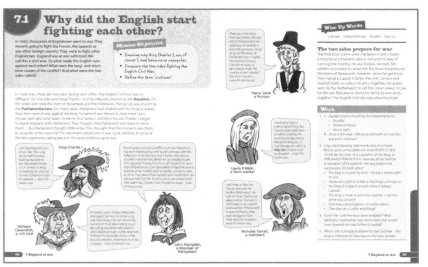

Renaissance, Revolution and Reformation pages 96–97

Lesson summary

Students will analyse the causes of the English Civil War by writing an essay and acting out a television talk show. This lesson includes cross-curricular links to English, Religious Education, and Drama.

What are the lesson outcomes?

All students will answer questions about, and write an essay describing, the causes of the Civil War.

Most students will write an essay explaining why the Civil War was caused by the king and/or Parliament.

Some students will categorize and analyse the causes of the Civil War.

	I can identify causes of the Civil War.
	I can describe causes of the Civil War.
	I can explain why either the king or Parliament was to blame for the Civil War.
	I can explain why both the king and Parliament were to blame for the Civil War.
	I can analyse the causes of the Civil War by deciding whether it was mainly the king's or Parliament's fault.

Task 4: Students should act out a television chat show in which Charles I and his supporters are confronted by Parliament about their grievances.

How will students demonstrate their understanding?

In **Task 1** students formulate and refine their ideas, ready to complete Work activity **4**. Writing an essay will allow students to demonstrate their abilities to identify, describe, explain, evaluate, and analyse causation.

Starter suggestion

- Students could be asked to make a list of all the wars they have heard of. Ask them who was fighting in each example and/or what they have in common. This provides a way in to explaining the difference between international and civil wars.

Main learning suggestions and assessment

What activities will take place?

Task 1: Students should read pages 96–97 and complete Work activities **1–4** and 7.1 Civil War Worksheet.

Task 2: To expand Work activity **4**, students should write an essay answering the question 'Which side was mostly to blame for the Civil War?' Students could use 7.1 Cause and Consequence History Skills Activity to hold a class debate in preparation for this essay.

Task 3: Using the following tick list, students should peer-assess each other's work. They should then return to their own essays and be given time to improve them.

Plenary suggestions

- Students could be shown 'speech bubbles' (similar to those found on pages 96-97) and asked whether they belong to a supporter of the king or of Parliament. Students could move to different sides of the room to indicate who they think each 'speech bubble' belongs to.

Differentiation suggestions

Support

- In **Task 2** lower ability students could be given a writing frame that includes sentence starters to scaffold their ideas.

Extension: Hungry for more?

- The most able students could complete a Venn diagram in which they categorize the causes of the Civil War into political, economic, or religious factors (or a combination of these).

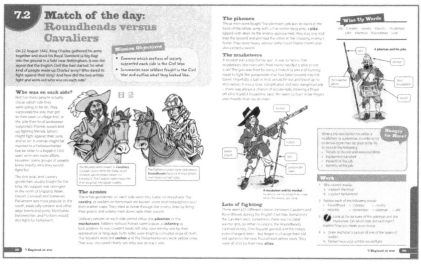

Renaissance, Revolution and Reformation pages 98–99

Lesson summary

Students will conduct a historical enquiry and plan their own historical re-enactment. This lesson includes opportunities for students to develop critical thinking skills.

What are the lesson outcomes?

All students will select and categorize information about the Civil War.

Most students will use evidence to explain the strengths and/or weaknesses of each side in the Civil War.

Some students will use evidence and critical thinking skills to decide which side was most likely to win the Civil War.

Starter suggestion

- Students should create a short 'call to arms' for the Royalists or Parliamentarians, explaining why people should fight for them.

Main learning suggestions and assessment

What activities will take place?

Task 1: Students should read pages 98–99 and use the information to complete Work activities **1–5**. They should also complete 7.2 Soldiers Worksheets 1 and 2, which ask students to identify the features and qualities of Civil War soldiers.

Task 2: Students will consider different aspects of the information they are given in order to complete a historical enquiry. Students should 'wear' different coloured 'hats', from the following list. At the end of this enquiry students should be asked which side in the Civil War they think was the strongest and why.

White	Facts: data and information
Red	Emotions: how did each side feel?

Yellow	Strengths that each side might have had
Black	Problems that each side might have had
Green	Creative thinking: how could each side improve their chances of winning?
Blue	Processing: working out which side was the most likely to win the war.

Task 3: Students should pretend that they have been asked to stage a re-enactment of a Civil War battle. They need to design costumes and make a list of props.

Task 4: Students should watch 7.2 Brothers Film Clip and complete 7.2 Film Worksheet.

Task 5: Students should complete 7.2 Enquiry History Skills Activity, explaining the differences between Cavaliers and Roundheads.

How will students demonstrate their understanding?

In **Task 2**, students use their critical thinking skills to work out which side was stronger. In **Tasks 3** and **5** students select and summarize relevant information.

Plenary suggestions

- Students should explain which side they think was stronger and why.

Differentiation suggestions

Support

- In **Task 2**, lower ability students could be asked to wear the white and red 'hats'; core students could consider the yellow and black 'hats'.

Extension: Hungry for more?

- Students could research which side people in their local area were on during the Civil War. They could research a local Civil War battleground or stronghold such as a castle.

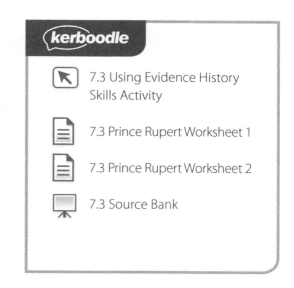

Renaissance, Revolution and Reformation pages 100–101

Lesson summary

Students will analyse sources and complete formative assessment questions about the sources.

What are the lesson outcomes?

All students will identify the meaning of two sources about Prince Rupert.

Most students will use evidence from the sources to explain their meaning and purpose.

Some students will use evidence from the sources and their contextual knowledge in order to explain the meaning and purpose of the sources.

Starter suggestion

- Students could annotate a copy of **Source D** by labelling the features they spot.

Main learning suggestions and assessment

What activities will take place?

Task 1: Students should read pages 100–101 and use the information to complete Work activities **1–4**.

Task 2: Students should then be asked what the purpose of **Source B** is, and peer-assess each other's work. They can create their own success criteria.

Task 3: Students should be asked 'What is the message of **Source C**? Use your own knowledge and detail from the source to explain your answer'. They could be given some success criteria, or asked to make their own based on what they think a good answer would contain.

Task 4: Students should complete 7.3 Using Evidence History Skills Activity.

How will students demonstrate their understanding?

In the starter activity students break down a visual source in order to give them the confidence to tackle more complex source work later in the lesson. **Tasks 2** and **3** enable students to develop skills for analysing sources, which are particularly valuable for developing the skills required at Key Stage 4. The plenary activity will help students to consolidate the skills developed in **Tasks 2** and **3**.

Plenary suggestions

- Students could be given an exemplar answer about the meaning or purpose of **Source D**, and asked how they could improve it.

Differentiation suggestions

Support

- In **Tasks 2** and **3**, lower ability students could be given success criteria, whilst higher ability students might be asked to consider for themselves what a 'good' and 'best' response would include.

- 7.3 Prince Rupert Worksheet 1 provides an alternative template for the source analysis in this lesson.

Extension: Hungry for more?

- An important aspect of Key Stage 4 History is the ability to examine the historiography of an event or individual. Students could be asked to research different historians and what they have written about Prince Rupert.

- Students could use 7.3 Prince Rupert Worksheet 2 to design a 'Wanted' poster for Prince Rupert. They should use what they now know about Roundhead propaganda to inform their work. An example 'Wanted' poster can be found on page 143 of the *Student Book*.

7.4 What was new about the New Model Army?

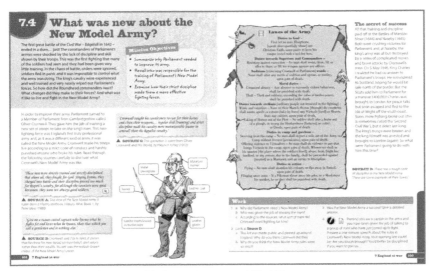

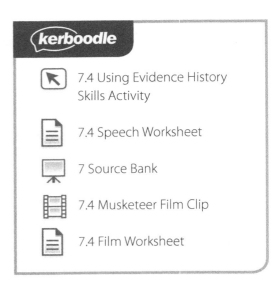

Renaissance, Revolution and Reformation pages 102–103

Lesson summary

Students will analyse a historian's interpretation of why the New Model Army was successful.

What are the lesson outcomes?

All students will identify why the historian Peter Moss thinks the New Model Army was so successful.

Most students will use contextual knowledge to explain a historical interpretation.

Some students will explain why Moss has made these conclusions, using what they know about contemporary beliefs and events to put his interpretation in context.

Starter suggestion

- Students could consolidate their knowledge of the soldiers on both sides at the start of the Civil War by labelling images of a musketeer and pikeman .

Main learning suggestions and assessment

What activities will take place?

Task 1: Students should read pages 102–103 and use the information to complete Work activities **1–4**.

Task 2: Students should create a 'before' and 'after' magazine article. They should describe the Parliamentarian army at the start of the Civil War, and again once the New Model Army was introduced.

Task 3: Students should develop their ability to analyse historical interpretations by focusing on **Source A** and considering the following: What does Peter Moss think were the New Model Army's three main strengths?; Do they agree with Moss? What evidence can they find to support this interpretation?; What might it be about modern life that makes many modern historians side with the Parliamentarians rather than Charles I? 7.4 Using Evidence History Skills Activity could also be used to examine the sources in this lesson.

Task 4: Students should watch 7.4 Musketeer Film Clip and complete 7.4 Film Worksheet.

How will students demonstrate their understanding?

In **Task 2** students will develop the ability to compare and contrast ideas. This is a skill that is examined at Key Stage 4, so introducing and refining these skills at Key Stage 3 is incredibly valuable. In **Task 3** students are asked to demonstrate their ability to evaluate the ideas of a modern historian. They identify and describe Peter Moss's interpretation, and use historical evidence to explain why Moss has created this interpretation. They also consider the modern beliefs that might inform this interpretation.

Plenary suggestions

- Students could use **Source D** to make their own list of rules for a classroom today. Are any of the rules that Cromwell imposed important for successful learning? Why?

Differentiation suggestions

Support

- In **Task 2** students could be given the option of how to present their ideas, such as in a written magazine article or as a dramatic performance.

Extension: Hungry for more?

- Students could further research the Battle of Marsden Moor and the Battle of Naseby, in order to fully analyse the tactics used by the New Model Army and why these tactics led them to success in the Civil War.

- Students could complete 7.4 Speech Worksheet for homework.

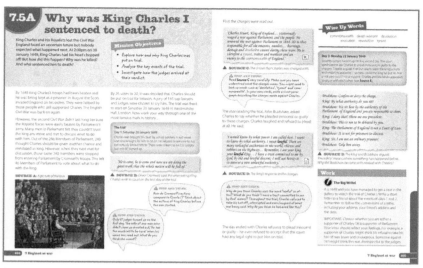

Renaissance, Revolution and Reformation pages 104–105

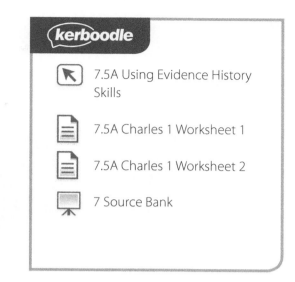

Lesson summary

Students will use different writing styles to create empathetic and biased accounts of the first two days of Charles' trial. This lesson includes cross-curricular links to English (different styles of writing).

What are the lesson outcomes?

All students will use empathy and bias to create an account of Charles' trial, from the perspective of a Royalist or a Parliamentarian.

Most students will use contextual knowledge and a variety of sources to explain why Charles believed Parliament could not try him.

Some students will use and analyse sources, testing their reliability and making inferences from them, in order to decide whether or not it was inevitable that Charles was found guilty.

Starter suggestion

- Students could makes notes on a defence for Charles, listing anything they think proves that he is innocent or proves that Parliament was to blame for the Civil War.

Main learning suggestions and assessment

What activities will take place?

Task 1: Students should read pages 104–105 and complete 7.5A Charles I Worksheet 1, which asks them to consider quotations from the trial. They should then complete the Work activity, in which they will write a biased letter from either a Royalist or a Parliamentarian.

Task 2: Students should make a list or spider diagram of words to describe how they think Charles might be feeling after the first two days of his trial. In a class discussion

afterwards students could explain why they chose each word.

Task 3: Students should use the words that they identified in **Task 2** to write either an entry in Charles' diary or a letter from him to his wife, Henrietta Maria.

Task 4: Students should create a newspaper report about the first two days of Charles' trial, documenting the events and Charles' responses to the charges.

How will students demonstrate their understanding?

Students use empathy to describe how Charles would have felt and identify bias within an account. This enables students to understand the nature of bias and be better able to spot it in sources, so they can analyse how useful and reliable sources are when conducting a historical enquiry.

Plenary suggestions

- Students could complete 7.5A Using Evidence History Skills Activity to consolidate their learning.

Differentiation suggestions

Support

- In **Task 3**, students could be given an example of a diary to help model the task. This could be about a football match, for example. In the example there should be evidence of bias ('the stupid ref was blind!') and of emotive language which students can pick out.

Extension: Hungry for more?

- Students could research Charles' time in Carisbrooke Castle. They could consider why they think this site was chosen as Charles' prison, what Charles' life was like there, and what evidence we can still find at the castle today about the events of the time.

- Students could complete 7.5A Charles II Worksheet 2 as homework.

7.5B Why was King Charles I sentenced to death?

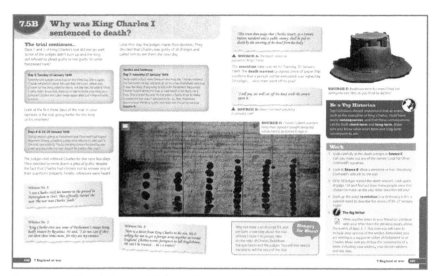

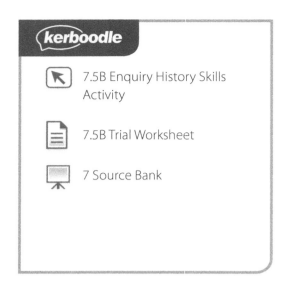

Renaissance, Revolution and Reformation pages 106–107

Lesson summary

Students will test a historical interpretation using their own knowledge and by analysing sources. This lesson includes cross-curricular links to English (writing a formal letter).

What are the lesson outcomes?

All students will use empathy and bias to create an account of Charles' trial, from the perspective of a Royalist or a Parliamentarian.

Most students will use contextual knowledge and a variety of sources to explain why Charles believed Parliament could not try him.

Some students will use and analyse sources, testing their reliability and making inferences from them, in order to decide whether or not it was inevitable that Charles was found guilty.

Starter suggestion

- Students could consolidate their knowledge from the previous lesson by writing three short social networking posts for Charles I about the first two days of his trial.

Main learning suggestions and assessment

What activities will take place?

Task 1: Students should read pages 106–107 and complete Work activities **1–5** and 7.5B Trial Worksheet.

Task 2: Students could be introduced to the historiography of the late nineteenth century, when some historians, such as S.R. Gardiner, believed that many of the signatures on Charles' death warrant were signed before the verdict was delivered. Students could be asked if they can find any evidence in Cromwell's attitude to support this interpretation.

Task 3: Students should pretend to be one of the judges who refused to sign Charles' death warrant. They should write a letter to Cromwell and Bradshaw explaining their decision.

Task 4: Students should complete 7.5B Enquiry History Skills Activity.

How will students demonstrate their understanding?

In **Tasks 1** and **2**, students will consider how fair Charles' trail was and whether there is any evidence to suggest that it was inevitable that he was found guilty by making inferences from sources. In **Task 3** students will apply their conclusions about the inevitability of the verdict, coupled with their contextual knowledge about why some contemporaries believed that the trial was illegal.

Plenary suggestions

- Students could be told that after Charles' death, Parliament demanded that his executioner return his death warrant (**Source C**). It has been in their archives ever since. This could be used as a catalyst for a class discussion about the significance of this document and why it might be so important to politicians even five centuries after these events occurred.

Differentiation suggestions

Support

- In **Task 2**, it may not be appropriate to use the references to the historiography around Charles' death warrant with all students.

Extension: Hungry for more?

- There is evidence that the death warrant has been altered, with names scratched off and words changed. Students could research what changes have been made and when, why they were made, and what implications they have regarding what we know about the trial and the reliability of the source.

7.6 Charlie for the chop!

Renaissance, Revolution and Reformation pages 108–109

Lesson summary
Students will complete an assessment in which they write an obituary for Charles I. This lesson includes cross-curricular links to English (writing in different styles/writing to inform).

What are the lesson outcomes?
All students will select and summarize information about Charles I in order to write an obituary.

Most students will use their prior knowledge to describe the life and death of Charles I.

Some students will use their prior knowledge and a critical analysis of a range of sources to explain different aspects and interpretations of the life and death of Charles I.

Starter suggestion
- Students could be shown a copy of **Source B** on page 109 or in 7 Source Bank and asked to play 'I Spy' with a partner to identify five things they can see in the picture. Then they should pretend that it is to be published in a newspaper report about the execution of Charles and that they are the editor who must come up with a caption for the picture.

Main learning suggestions and assessment
What activities will take place?
Task 1: Students should read pages 108–109 and use the information to complete Work activities **1–4**.

Task 2: Students should write an obituary for Charles I as an assessment. This should include his greatest achievements (if any!), the mistakes he made, and details about his trial and death.

Task 3: Students should complete 7.6 Using History Skills Activity.

How will students demonstrate their understanding?
In **Task 1**, students are able to refine their ideas about the death of Charles I and use sources in a critical manner in order to answer questions. They need to develop these skills in order to write their obituary in **Task 2**. They should use contextual knowledge and a range of sources to explain, evaluate, and analyse ideas.

Plenary suggestions
- Students could use the charges against Charles and what they know about Parliament's complaints about him as a leader to create a manifesto for Oliver Cromwell. This should set out how the country will be led after Charles' death.

Differentiation suggestions
Support
- In **Task 2**, lower ability students could be given a list of questions to answer in their work.

Extension: Hungry for more?
- In this chapter the predominant interpretation of Charles I is that he was a weak king. Students could now use the information about Charles' execution to attempt to build a counter-interpretation in which they celebrate Charles as a brave, courageous, and pious leader. They could produce a piece of work in which they design a front cover and blurb for their own history book entitled 'Charles the Hero!'

- Students could use 7.6 Journalism Worksheets 1 and 2 to design their own front page newspaper coverage of the execution.

Overview:
Chapter 8 Cromwell's Commonwealth

Helping you deliver KS3 History National Curriculum

Both the Interregnum (including Cromwell in Ireland) and the Restoration are specifically mentioned as example topics in the KS3 History National Curriculum for 2014. The concepts, content, and historical terminology can be quite challenging, so the lessons in this chapter break the topics down simply, neatly, and logically while giving students plenty of opportunity to demonstrate their understanding. Students are required to offer opinions, come to their own conclusions, sort through a variety of sources and evidence, and use their findings to support their answers. Higher-level concepts such as significance and interpretations are covered, and students use their writing to explore and develop their ideas as well as organize and structure their work in order to write appropriate answers.

The Big Picture

Why are we teaching 'Cromwell's Commonwealth'?

This chapter investigates the life and times of one of British history's most divisive figures – Oliver Cromwell. The opening lesson – and its immediate hook about the banning of Christmas – examines Cromwell's Commonwealth and requires students to define some advanced historical terminology. We then ask students to evaluate one of the most infamous and far-reaching episodes in Anglo-Irish relations – Cromwell's invasion of Ireland. His reputation is further put under the spotlight in the next lesson as we analyse why one man can be both so admired and so reviled, and students are required to make their own judgements.

Skills and processes covered in this chapter

		8.1	8.2	8.3	8.4A	8.4B
History skills	Historical enquiry		✓			
	Using evidence and source work		✓		✓	✓
	Chronological understanding	✓			✓	✓
	Understanding cultural, ethnic and religious diversity	✓	✓		✓	
	Change and continuity	✓			✓	
	Cause and consequence	✓			✓	✓
	Significance	✓		✓		
	Interpretations		✓	✓		
	Making links/connections		✓		✓	✓
	Explores similarities and differences	✓		✓		
Literacy and numeracy	Key words identified/deployed	✓	✓		✓	✓
	Extended writing		✓			
	Encourages reading for meaning	✓	✓	✓	✓	✓
	Focuses on structuring writing					
	Asks students to use writing to explore and develop ideas	✓	✓	✓		✓
	Learn through talk/discussion		✓			
	Numeracy opportunities					
Activity types	Creative task	✓		✓		✓
	Emphasizes role of individual	✓	✓	✓	✓	
	Group work					✓
	Independent research					
	Develops study skills	✓	✓	✓		

The chapter ends with the kind of historical anecdote that students love – that is, the gory tale of Cromwell's head! There are few people in history whose stories continue to such a degree after their deaths. By investigating just what happened to Cromwell's skull, students are not only taken on a journey through 400 years of British history, they also consider the immediate events that saw the return of the monarchy.

Lesson sequence

Lesson title	NC references	Objectives	Outcomes
8.1 The man who banned Christmas pp110–111	The Interregnum (including Cromwell in Ireland)	• Define the words 'republic' and 'interregnum'. • Discover how the country changed under Cromwell. • Explain why Christmas was banned.	**All** students will complete a historical enquiry in which they answer questions to describe how different Cromwell was from Charles I. **Most** students will complete a historical enquiry, explaining why Cromwell was different from Charles I. **Some** students will analyse the extent to which England became a true republic during the Interregnum.
8.2 Cromwell: curse of Ireland? pp112–113	The Interregnum (including Cromwell in Ireland)	• Recall how Cromwell is viewed in Ireland. • Analyse what he did to earn his reputation in Ireland. • Judge whether he deserves his terrible reputation.	**All** students will match evidence to statements about Cromwell. **Most** students will describe Cromwell's actions that led to him being given the title, the 'curse of Ireland'. **Some** students will analyse information to explain whether or not Cromwell deserves to be called the 'curse of Ireland'.
8.3 Cromwell: hero or villain? pp114–115	The Interregnum (including Cromwell in Ireland)	• Examine why people admired and respected Cromwell. • Examine why others disliked him. • Judge whether you think Cromwell was a hero or a villain.	**All** students will categorize evidence by deciding which interpretation it supports. **Most** students will analyse interpretations and decide whether Cromwell was a hero or a villain. **Some** students will use their knowledge of historical events and the wider contemporary world in order to suggest why different interpretations arise.
8.4A Whatever happened to Cromwell's head? pp116–117 **8.4B Whatever happened to Cromwell's head? pp118–119**	The Interregnum (including Cromwell in Ireland) The Restoration	• Define the word 'regicide'. • Explain why the country became a monarchy once more. • Explain how and why King Charles II sought revenge after 1660.	**All** students will describe what England was like when Charles II returned. **Most** students will explain how much political change occurred between 1649 and 1660. **Some** students will decide how much change the English Civil War really caused and, therefore, the nature of the definition of the word 'revolution' in this context.

Ideas for enrichment

Ask students to investigate other divisive figures in history. Margaret Thatcher, Richard III, and Neville Chamberlain are good examples. This is a very challenging task that will certainly stretch your high achievers.

Cromwell's statue sits outside Parliament today. What about the other statues outside Parliament – who are they? And what about the statues inside? You could set students questions such as 'Why do people have statues built of them?', 'Who decides to put statues up?', or even 'Do any statues of evil people exist?'.

Set students a challenge of investigating the life and times of the Major-General in charge of the area where they live.

Ask students to think about what Cromwell's reputation in Ireland might be today. Do any of them have relatives living in Ireland, or have links to Ireland? Can they find out about Cromwell's reputation?

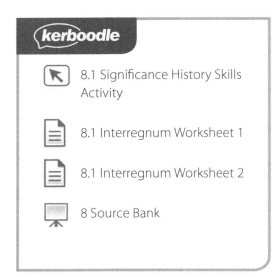

Renaissance, Revolution and Reformation pages 110–111

Lesson summary

Students will conduct a historical enquiry, in which they will use their own knowledge about Charles I and independent research to analyse how much change occurred under Cromwell. This lesson includes critical thinking and independent enquiry skills.

What are the lesson outcomes?

All students will complete a historical enquiry in which they answer questions to describe how different Cromwell was from Charles I.

Most students will complete a historical enquiry, explaining why Cromwell was different from Charles I.

Some students will analyse the extent to which England became a true republic during the Interregnum.

Starter suggestion

- As an introduction to the chapter, show students the 'warts and all' portrait of Cromwell in 8 Source Bank and tell them about his instructions to the artist. Students could make inferences about the kind of leader they think Cromwell might have been. Remind them of how Elizabeth controlled portraits of herself.

Main learning suggestions and assessment

What activities will take place?

Task 1: Students should read pages 110–111 and use the information to complete Work activities **1–3**.

Task 2: Students should compare England under Cromwell with what it had been like under Charles I. To conduct a fully independent enquiry, students should come up with some questions to help focus their investigation.

Task 3: Students should pretend to be Lucy Hutchinson and complete her letter to Cromwell explaining why people did not like his puritanical rule. Alternatively, students could make a 'secret' Christmas card that mocks Cromwell and his Puritan ways.

Task 4: Students should complete 8.1 Significance History Skills Activity, which analyses the impact of Cromwell's rule. They should also complete 8.1 Interregnum Worksheets 1 and 2.

How will students demonstrate their understanding?

In **Task 2**, students will develop enquiry skills by devising relevant questions, independently researching information, critically using and evaluating sources, and reaching and supporting sustained conclusions.

Plenary suggestions

- Following the completion of their enquiry, students could be asked, 'Was Cromwell really any different from Charles I?' This could take the form of a discussion within small groups or a written answer.

Differentiation suggestions

Support

- In **Task 2**, lower ability students should be given the following questions to consider for each of the two men: How well did he get on with Parliament? Could he/did he rule without Parliament? What clothes did he wear? Who would rule after him? Could he decide what religion the country should be?

Extension: Hungry for more?

- Students could research historical interpretations of Cromwell. They should find examples of historians who saw him as a true democratic leader and those who thought that his rule was similar to the rule of a king.

8.2 Cromwell: curse of Ireland?

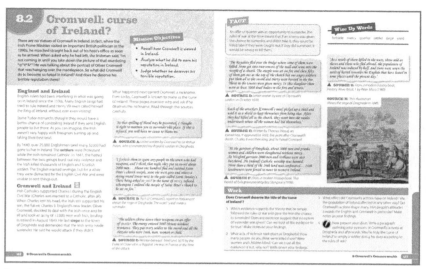

Renaissance, Revolution and Reformation pages 112–113

Lesson summary

Students will use evidence to answer questions for an enquiry into an interpretation of Cromwell. This lesson includes cross-curricular links to English (different styles of writing).

What are the lesson outcomes?

All students will match evidence to statements about Cromwell.

Most students will describe Cromwell's actions that led to him being given the title, the 'curse of Ireland'.

Some students will analyse information to explain whether or not Cromwell deserves to be called the 'curse of Ireland'.

Starter suggestion

- Students could be asked to write five rules for soldiers to follow during a war, to help them decide what is fair and what is not.

Main learning suggestions and assessment

What activities will take place?

Task 1: Students should read pages 112–113 and complete Work activities **1–4** and 8.2 Cromwell Worksheet 1. In this worksheet, students write a letter as if they were a soldier in Cromwell's army at Drogheda.

Task 2: Students should refer back to the starter activity and, next to each of their rules, give an example of whether or not Cromwell followed this rule.

Task 3: Students should imagine that they are Bertie Ahern, the Irish prime minister in 1997. Ahern has just marched out

of the office of the British foreign minister (Robin Cook). They should write a note explaining why Ahern was so offended by the portrait of Cromwell in Cook's office.

Task 4: Students should complete 8.2 Using Evidence History Skills Activity, where they develop the skill of using evidence to support their explanations. They could also use 8.2 Cromwell Worksheet 2 to organize a class debate.

How will students demonstrate their understanding?

Tasks 1, **2** and the plenary activity ask students to weigh up evidence supporting two interpretations, before analysing and evaluating to reach a final conclusion.

Plenary suggestions

- Watch 8.2 Drogheda Mini-Movie with the class and then explain that Cromwell justified his actions at Drogheda. He said that it saved lives, as other Irish towns and garrisons were then so scared of the English that they surrendered without a fight. A class discussion about whether this really made his actions justifiable could then take place.

Differentiation suggestions

Support

- In the starter activity, lower ability students could be given a list of rules and asked to choose the five that they think are most important. This will help them focus their ideas so that they are useful in **Task 2**.

Extension: Hungry for more?

- Cromwell believed that he was 'God's executioner'. Students could find examples that suggest that he had people killed in the name of God or because they had different religious views from himself.

8.3 Cromwell: hero or villain?

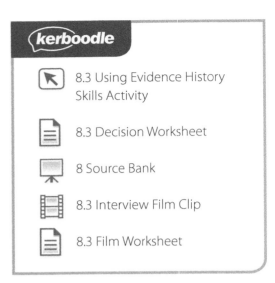

Renaissance, Revolution and Reformation pages 114–115

Lesson summary

Students will examine different interpretations of Cromwell, in order to analyse whether he was a hero or a villain, in a piece of extended writing.

What are the lesson outcomes?

All students will categorize evidence by deciding which interpretation it supports.

Most students will analyse interpretations and decide whether Cromwell was a hero or a villain.

Some students will use their knowledge of historical events and the wider contemporary world in order to suggest why different interpretations arise.

Starter suggestion

- Students could write a reference for Cromwell, either recommending him for a job or explaining why he should not be employed. They should use what they know about him, his role as Lord protector, his religious beliefs, and his actions in Ireland.

Main learning suggestions and assessment

What activities will take place?

Task 1: Students should read pages 114–115 and use the information to complete Work activities **1–3**. To develop Work activities **1a** and **b**, students could draw round their hand twice and label one 'hero' and the other 'villain'. They then could write a point of view on each finger as evidence to support each interpretation. This will help students to consider two sides of an argument (on one hand… but on the other hand…).

Task 2: To develop Work activity **2**, students could be asked to write an essay in which they analyse the different interpretations of Cromwell.

Task 3: Students should complete 8.3 Using Evidence History Skills Activity in which they analyse a historical interpretation.

Task 4: Students should watch 8.3 Interview Film Clip and then complete 8.3 Film Worksheet.

How will students demonstrate their understanding?

Task 1 enables students to organize their ideas and plan their work. In **Task 2**, depending on their ability, students may be: recalling; identifying; describing; explaining; evaluating; and/or analysing information within a historical enquiry.

Plenary suggestions

- Show **Source A** in the source bank for this chapter and ask students to explain why they think Cromwell's statue stands outside the House of Commons. Why is he so significant to Parliament? What interpretation of Cromwell does it support? Why? What groups of people might disagree with this interpretation? Why?

Differentiation suggestions

Support

- In **Task 1**, lower ability students could be given typed up interpretations of Cromwell so that their task becomes sorting these onto the correct hand, rather than summarizing and writing each argument out.

- In **Task 2**, students could instead complete 8.3 Decision Worksheet, which scaffolds their response.

Extension: Hungry for more?

- Students could investigate different historians and/ or schools of history and what their interpretation of Cromwell is. For example, they could research the Whig school of history, what historians who subscribe to it think about Cromwell, and why this is likely to be.

8.4A Whatever happened to Cromwell's head?

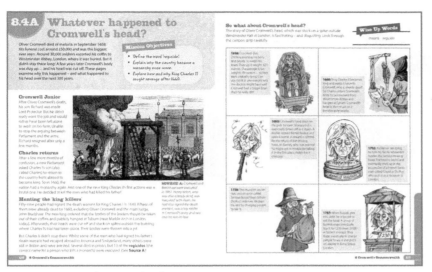

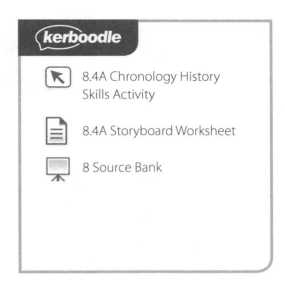

Renaissance, Revolution and Reformation pages 116–117

Lesson summary

Students will learn about the changes that occurred in England after the death of Cromwell and decide what he would have thought about them.

What are the lesson outcomes?

All students will describe what England was like when Charles II returned.

Most students will explain how much political change occurred between 1649 and 1660.

Some students will decide how much change the English Civil War really caused and, therefore, the nature of the definition of the word 'revolution' in this context.

Starter suggestion

- Students could be told that in 1660 Charles II returned to England and became king. They could then complete a 'to do' list for him, by deciding what he might want to change about how the country was being run.

Main learning suggestions and assessment

What activities will take place?

Task 1: Students should read page 116. They should imagine that they work for Parliament in 1660; following Richard Cromwell's resignation, they have been asked to write a letter to Charles II, asking him to become king.

Task 2: Students should then write a document briefing Charles II about England during the years that Cromwell was Lord Protector, so that he knows what problems he faces.

Task 3: Students should create a 'wanted' poster for Charles I's regicides. This should include details about who the most wanted men were (Cromwell and Bradshaw) and what they have done.

Task 4: Students should write an obituary for Oliver Cromwell, either for the 'Royalist Review' or 'Government Gazette'. In this they should present a biased interpretation, summarizing everything they know about Cromwell. This could be used as a summative assessment.

How will students demonstrate their understanding?

This lesson allows students to demonstrate their ability to identify, describe, explain, and make inferences about events. **Task 1** is a comprehension activity, but also allows some students to consider the nature and responsibilities of leadership. In *8.1 The man who banned Christmas* students started to consider how 'kingly' Cromwell was and this activity allows them to use those ideas to explain to Charles II what kind of kingdom he is taking over. Students are also able to consider how much change, continuity, progression, and regression had occurred.

Plenary suggestions

- Students could complete 8.4A Chronology History Skills Activity to consolidate their learning.

Differentiation suggestions

Support

- In **Task 2**, lower ability students could be given information about Cromwell's reign. They can use this to describe why the people of England are unhappy and what immediate problems Charles needs to solve.

Extension: Hungry for more?

- Charles II had thirteen regicides executed. Students will know of Cromwell and Bradshaw, but they could research the others and their role in the execution of Charles I.

- Students could complete 8.4A Storyboard Worksheet as homework.

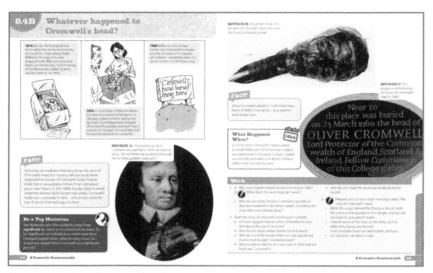

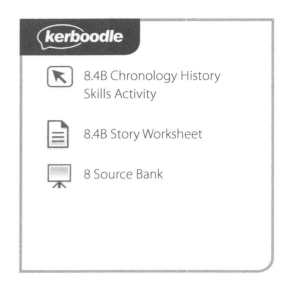

Renaissance, Revolution and Reformation pages 118–119

Lesson summary

Students will learn about the changes that occurred in England after the death of Cromwell and decide what he would have thought about them. This lesson includes cross-curricular links to Mathematics (creating a line graph and basic chronology).

What are the lesson outcomes?

All students will describe what England was like when Charles II returned.

Most students will explain how much political change occurred between 1649 and 1660.

Some students will decide how much change the English Civil War really caused and, therefore, the nature of the definition of the word 'revolution' in this context.

Starter suggestion

- Students could create their own wordsearch puzzles using key words from throughout the chapter. Once these are complete, they could swap with a partner and try to solve each other's puzzle.

Main learning suggestions and assessment

What activities will take place?

Task 1: Having read pages 116–119 over this and the previous lesson, students should use the information to complete Work activities **1–3**.

Task 2: Students should create a 'living graph' charting what Cromwell would have thought about the key events of his life… and death! They should be provided with either a list of key dates and events or typed up captions to stick on their graph to show how Cromwell would have felt at each time.

Task 3: Students should pretend to be Samuel Russell, and create an advert telling people about their opportunity to see Cromwell's head. The advert should say why Cromwell is still a person of such interest, even in the next century.

Task 4: Students should complete 8.4B Chronology History Skills Activity.

Task 5: Students should complete 8.4B Story Worksheet, in which they must write a short story about what happened to Cromwell's head.

How will students demonstrate their understanding?

The cartoon on pages 117–118 will help students to establish a basic chronological framework of events. This will then be tested in **Task 2**. Students will also use empathy to decide how Cromwell would have felt about different events.

Plenary suggestions

- Students could be asked to consider the word 'revolution' and its different meanings: a sudden and violent change to power; or, travelling a full circle to return to where you started – like the revolution of a wheel. Ask them which they think is the better definition for the English Civil War. How much had things really changed by 1660?

Differentiation suggestions

Support

- In **Task 2**, students could be given shorter time frames to consider: Cromwell's death and what happened to his head, or Cromwell becoming Lord Protector until the burial of his head.

Extension: Hungry for more?

- Students could develop the plenary activity into an essay. This could be set as homework in order to encourage independent historical enquiry.

Overview: Chapter 9 The Restoration

Helping you deliver KS3 History National Curriculum

Any study of the period 1509 to 1745 must include a detailed examination of the Restoration era. Thankfully, it is a time in history filled with fascinating topics and captivating sources that allow students to become absorbed in the era.

There is certainly a lot for students to do as they work their way through this chapter. For example, they will be challenged to make links between different events and to show how one event can lead to another. They will have to identify new key terms and use them appropriately, assess the significance of events and individuals, and select and combine information from sources to complete tasks.

The Big Picture

Why are we teaching 'The Restoration'?

The chapter opens by exploring the comparatively hedonistic days of the Restoration that took place soon after the puritanical days of the Commonwealth. The contrast between the two eras is highlighted in the first lesson, which also asks students to define key terms, analyse a source in detail, and use their creative skills.

The next lessons cover the Great Plague – always a topic that engrosses students. Pepys' curious observations of London life and some bizarre plague remedies are outlined here. We then move on to the next key event of Restoration times – the Great Fire of London! Here, students are required to look in depth at the conditions that allowed the fire to sweep through the city, contemporary explanations of the cause, and the fire's importance in shaping the London of today.

Skills and processes covered in this chapter

		9.1	9.2	9.3	9.4A	9.4B	9.4C	9.5	9.6
History skills	Historical enquiry				✓	✓	✓		
	Using evidence and source work	✓	✓	✓	✓	✓		✓	
	Chronological understanding		✓		✓				
	Understanding cultural, ethnic and religious diversity	✓				✓		✓	
	Change and continuity	✓					✓		
	Cause and consequence		✓		✓	✓	✓		✓
	Significance	✓			✓		✓		
	Interpretations					✓			
	Making links/connections	✓	✓	✓			✓		
	Explores similarities and differences						✓	✓	✓
Literacy and numeracy	Key words identified/deployed	✓					✓	✓	✓
	Extended writing					✓			
	Encourages reading for meaning	✓	✓	✓	✓	✓	✓	✓	✓
	Focuses on structuring writing					✓			✓
	Asks students to use writing to explore and develop ideas	✓	✓	✓	✓	✓	✓	✓	
	Learn through talk/discussion	✓	✓		✓				✓
	Numeracy opportunities		✓	✓					
Activity types	Creative task	✓							✓
	Emphasizes role of individual	✓					✓		
	Group work	✓							✓
	Independent research			✓				✓	
	Develops study skills		✓			✓			

The lives of women in the Restoration era are then examined. We attempt to address why so little history of this period is shaped by the actions of women – particularly women of the lower classes. In our experience, it is not just female students who find the sexist nature of society during this period both alarming and fascinating.

The chapter closes with an intriguing spread where students consider the bizarre and brutal medical treatments of the period. A fun and engaging task about poor King Charles II helps to set up a later chapter which outlines some of the great scientific and technological advances of the later period.

Lesson sequence

Lesson title	NC references	Objectives	Outcomes
9.1 Who was the Merry Monarch? pp120–121	The Restoration	• Explore how, when and why Charles II became king. • Compare Cromwell's nation with the Merry Monarch's.	**All** students will use evidence to describe the Merry Monarch. **Most** students will explain why Charles II was known as the Merry Monarch. **Some** students will analyse how different Charles II was from Cromwell.
9.2 Bring out your dead! pp122–123	The Restoration	• Explore what people knew about the spread of plague and disease in seventeenth-century London.	**All** students will extract information from a source. **Most** students will use evidence from a variety of sources to support their descriptions. **Some** students will use evidence from a variety of sources to support their explanations.
9.3 Ring a ring o' roses pp124–125	The Restoration	• Recall the symptoms of the Great Plague. • Explore how a nursery rhyme tells us how people tried to avoid catching the plague.	**All** students will describe causes and symptoms of, and remedies for, plague. **Most** students will explain causes and symptoms of, and remedies for, plague. **Some** students will use empathetic understanding to explain what it would have been like living in London during the outbreak of plague in 1665.
9.4A Who started the Great Fire of London? pp126–127 **9.4B Who started the Great Fire of London? pp128–129** **9.4C Who started the Great Fire of London? pp130–131**	The Restoration	• Describe how the Great Fire devastated London. • Investigate how and why interpretations of the cause of the Great Fire have changed since 1666. • Evaluate how London was rebuilt after 1666.	**All** students will identify the problems with the poor housing in London prior to the Great Fire of London. **Most** students will explain why interpretations of the Great Fire of London have changed over time. **Some** students will explain why having to rebuild London was both a good thing and a bad thing.
9.5 What about the women? pp132–133	The Restoration	• Compare the lives of rich and poor women in Tudor and Stuart times. • Explore how some men treated their wives.	**All** students will use empathy to describe the experiences of women living in this era. **Most** students will use their own knowledge to put a source into its historical context. **Some** students will analyse how typical a source is, using evidence from the source and their own knowledge.
9.6 Can you cure King Charles II? pp134–135	The Restoration	• Evaluate the various treatments on offer to King Charles II and make decisions about what to do.	**All** students will make decisions about how to treat Charles II. **Most** students will use their prior knowledge of Renaissance medicine to make decisions about how to treat Charles II. **Some** students will explain why Renaissance medicine was often quite bizarre!

Ideas for enrichment

Students could carry out an extension project on the life and achievements of Sir Christopher Wren and the landmarks he designed.

In our experience, the tale of the Great Fire gets students to view the Fire Service in a new light. This can lead nicely to a research project on the history and evolution of the Fire Service and their equipment.

The Great Plague was a sudden outbreak of disease that killed thousands. Ask students to research other epidemics and pandemics. Can they remember hearing about any on the news, such as swine flu?

How about asking students to write a biography of Samuel Pepys? He was a fascinating character that some students may know about.

Charles II had many children – none of them by his wife. Ask students to find out what happened to his illegitimate offspring.

Renaissance, Revolution and Reformation pages 120–121

Lesson summary

Students will explain why Charles II became known as the Merry Monarch and analyse how much political change took place during the Restoration. This lesson includes a focus on literacy (writing for a particular audience and purpose).

What are the lesson outcomes?

All students will use evidence to describe the Merry Monarch.

Most students will explain why Charles II was known as the Merry Monarch.

Some students will analyse how different Charles II was from Cromwell.

Starter suggestion

- Students could write an 'urgent' email to Charles II, asking him to return to England and explaining why he is needed.

Main learning suggestions and assessment

What activities will take place?

Task 1: Students should read pages 120–121 and use the information to complete Work activities **1–5**.

Task 2: Students should analyse change and continuity between the rule of Cromwell and the rule of Charles II. Was there anything that was similar? Or was the Restoration a time of great change? They should then complete 9.1 Charles II Worksheet 1.

Task 3: Students should create a website dedicated to the Merry Monarch. They should decide what to include and, if possible, research some aspects further, such as: Charles' relationship with Parliament; Charles' own religious turmoil; the wars Charles fought; the founding of the Royal Society.

Task 4: Students should complete 9.1 Significance History Skills Activity in which they assess the significance of Charles II.

How will students demonstrate their understanding?

In **Task 1**, students will demonstrate their knowledge and understanding of the Restoration period and will use evidence to support and explain their ideas. These skills are consolidated in **Task 2**. In **Task 3** higher ability students may be able to start drawing out some elements of continuity, such as Cromwell and Charles II's shared views on religious freedom.

Plenary suggestions

- Students could pitch an idea for a coronation party, using their knowledge of Charles' likes and lifestyle in order to come up with a suitable event.

- Students could complete 9.1 Charles II Worksheet 2.

Differentiation suggestions

Support

- To support students in reaching a conclusion in **Task 2**: you could give them a 'change and continuity' table:

	Relationship with Parliament	Religion in England	People's free time
Cromwell			
Charles II			
Change or continuity?			

Extension: Hungry for more?

- Students could decide whether the nickname 'the Merry Monarch' was fair or whether it belittled Charles' achievements as king.

9.2 Bring out your dead!

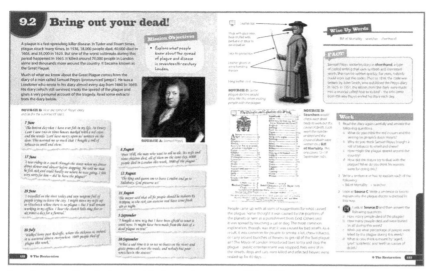

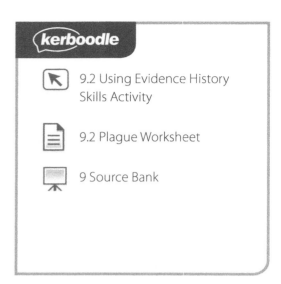

Renaissance, Revolution and Reformation pages 122–123

Lesson summary

Students will use evidence from a variety of sources in order to explain what people thought caused and cured plague in the seventeenth century. This lesson includes a focus on numeracy.

What are the lesson outcomes?

All students will extract information from a source.

Most students will use evidence from a variety of sources to support their descriptions.

Some students will use evidence from a variety of sources to support their explanations.

Starter suggestion

- Students could be shown an image of a plague doctor (such as **Source C** on page 123) and asked what they think it is. They should try to use evidence from the source to explain their ideas, for example, making inferences about why this person is carrying a stick.

Main learning suggestions and assessment

What activities will take place?

Task 1: Students should read pages 122–123 and use the information to complete Work activities **1–4**. To develop numeracy skills, students could be asked to create a pie chart showing the main causes of death according to **Source D**.

Task 2: Students should create a leaflet advising people about what causes plague and what they can do to avoid getting it.

Task 3: Students should complete 9.2 Using Evidence History Skills Activity in which they consider how useful a Bill of Mortality is to a historian.

How will students demonstrate their understanding?

In **Tasks 1** and **2**, most students will be able to cite evidence from sources to support their ideas. In **Task 3**, students decide and explain how useful a source is to a historian. In doing this they will demonstrate their ability to evaluate a source with reference to its historical context, and also by identifying and explaining its limitations.

Plenary suggestions

- Show students words and/or images associated with this lesson and ask them to find connections. For example, an image of a cat could link with a picture of Saturn, because people thought they were both possible causes of plague.

Differentiation suggestions

Support

- In **Task 2** students could be given typed up 'cause' and 'cure' cards to categorize prior to making their leaflets.

- In **Task 3** students could be given a step-by-step guide on how to answer a question about a source. They should aim to explain what the source is about, using both evidence from the source itself and their contextual knowledge. They should also think about what the source does not tell a historian about the plague.

Extension: Hungry for more?

- Students could conduct research to find out the meanings of the different causes of death identified in **Source D**.

- Students could complete 9.2 Plague Worksheet as homework. This worksheet assesses their understanding of the lesson and includes a focus on numeracy.

9.3 Ring a ring o' roses

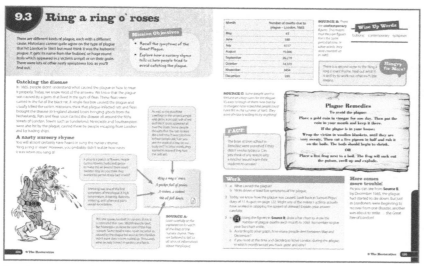

Renaissance, Revolution and Reformation pages 124–125

9.3 Cause and Consequence History Skills Activity

9.3 Symptoms Worksheet 1

9.3 Symptoms Worksheet 2

9 Source Bank

Lesson summary

Students will explore the meaning of the nursery rhyme 'Ring a ring o' roses' and create a scripted dialogue. This lesson includes a focus on numeracy (creating and reading a bar graph).

What are the lesson outcomes?

All students will describe causes and symptoms of, and remedies for, plague.

Most students will explain causes and symptoms of, and remedies for, plague.

Some students will use empathetic understanding to explain what it would have been like living in London during the outbreak of plague in 1665.

Starter suggestion

- Students could solve anagrams in order to reinforce their understanding of key words.

Main learning suggestions and assessment

What activities will take place?

Task 1: Students should read pages 124–125 and use the information to complete Work activities **1–3** and 9.3 Symptoms Worksheet 1.

Task 2: Students should work in pairs to write a scripted dialogue between a plague victim and a doctor. The victim should describe their symptoms and the doctor should recommend what the victim's family can do to stay safe.

Task 3: Students should pretend that they are Samuel Pepys living in London in 1665, and write a diary entry about what is happening and how it is making people feel.

Task 4: Students should complete 9.3 Cause and Consequence History Skills Activity.

How will students demonstrate their understanding?

Tasks 1 and **2** allow students to demonstrate their ability to recall, identify, describe, and explain contemporary beliefs about the causes of plague, its symptoms, and the suggested remedies. These skills are consolidated in **Task 3**, and some students will also be able to demonstrate their empathetic understanding by explaining how people might have felt about living through the plague.

Plenary suggestions

- Students could name obscure causes of plague, obscure symptoms or obscure remedies and share them with the class. The most obscure wins!

- Students could complete 9.3 Symptoms Worksheet 2 to consolidate their learning.

Differentiation suggestions

Support

- In **Task 2**, a script could be provided, in which the doctor asks questions to prompt the victim's answer. Halfway through, this swaps so that the victim asks questions about how they can keep their family safe.

- In work activity **3** students must draw a bar chart. It might be helpful for you to model this on the board so students are clear about what is expected of them.

Extension: Hungry for more?

- Students could be asked to research the scientific and, specifically, medical advancements made during the seventeenth century. They could focus on individuals such as William Harvey, Nicholas Culpeper, or Andreas Vesalius. This task is a good introduction to *9.6 Can you cure King Charles II?*

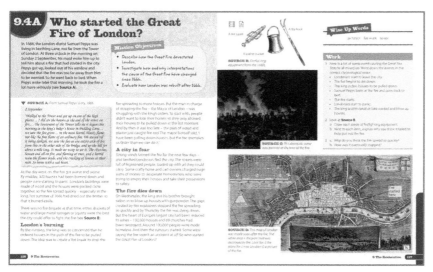

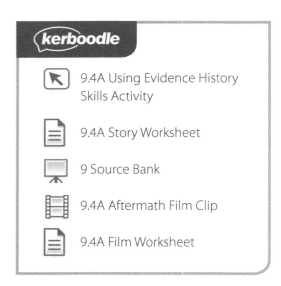

Renaissance, Revolution and Reformation pages 126–127

Lesson summary

Students will develop their understanding of cause and consequence by creating 'matching pairs' game cards.

What are the lesson outcomes?

All students will identify the problems with the poor housing in London prior to the Great Fire of London.

Most students will explain why interpretations of the Great Fire of London have changed over time.

Some students will explain why having to rebuild London was both a good thing and a bad thing.

Starter suggestion

- Students could be shown an extract of Pepys' diary from the day on which he buried his cheese in his garden. Ask them what they think might have led to such strange cheese storage ideas!

Main learning suggestions and assessment

What activities will take place?

Task 1: Students should read pages 126–127 and use the information to complete Work activities **1–3**.

Task 2: Students should consider cause and consequence by making and illustrating a set of 'matching pairs' cards. They should be given a set with either the cause or consequence for each pair already identified. For example:

Cause	Consequence
Some people believe there was an accident in a bakery in Pudding Lane.	The fire started.
London's buildings were made of wood.	They burned quickly and the fire spread faster.

Task 3: Once they have created their game cards, students should swap their set with another group. They should then have a game of 'matching pairs' in order to check each other's understanding of cause and consequence.

Task 4: Students should complete 9.4A Using Evidence History Skills Activity, which will develop their source analysis skills.

Task 5: Students should watch 9.4A Aftermath Film Clip and complete 9.4A Film Worksheet.

How will students demonstrate their understanding?

Task 2 encourages students to identify causes and consequences and then to explain how and why the Great Fire of London spread so quickly with such devastating consequences. In **Task 3** students check each other's understanding and, in doing so, consolidate their own.

Plenary suggestions

- Students could complete 9.4A Story Worksheet, which asks students to complete a piece of creative writing about the cause and spread of the fire.

Differentiation suggestions

Support

- In **Task 2**, lower ability students could be given a set of completed cause and consequence cards and be asked to match them.

Extension: Hungry for more?

- One of the consequences of the Great Fire of London was that insurance companies set up their own fire brigades. Students could be asked to research how these worked and create an advert for one of these schemes.

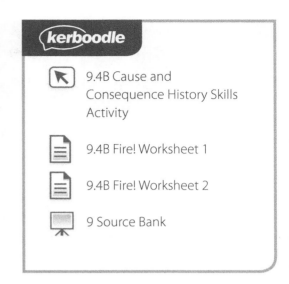

Renaissance, Revolution and Reformation pages 128–129

Lesson summary

Students will conduct an enquiry into why the Great Fire of London started and how interpretations of this event have changed over time.

What are the lesson outcomes?

All students will identify the problems with the poor housing in London prior to the Great Fire of London.

Most students will explain why interpretations of the Great Fire of London have changed over time.

Some students will explain why having to rebuild London was both a good thing and a bad thing.

Starter suggestion

- Students could be asked to match key words to their definitions. Key words could include: cause; consequence; interpretation; conspiracy; Catholic.

Main learning suggestions and assessment

What activities will take place?

Task 1: Students should read pages 128–129 and use the sources to complete a PEE (point, evidence, explanation) table, like the below.

Point	Evidence		Explanation
	Source	Quote	
People believed that Catholics had started the fire.			

Task 2: Students should make a timeline of interpretations, showing how ideas about the cause and spread of the fire have changed over time. To one side their timeline they should make notes about any historical context which may

have influenced a specific interpretation.

Task 3: Students should complete the enquiry in the Work activity. Both worksheets for this lesson support this enquiry.

Task 4: Students should complete 9.4B Cause and Consequence History Skills Activity. This activity asks students to consider the causes of the fire.

How will students demonstrate their understanding?

Tasks 1 and **2** help students to collate and refine their ideas and evidence, ready to complete **Task 3**. In **Task 3** students follow step-by-step guidance to complete an enquiry, and will be able to demonstrate their skills in: using evidence; explaining ideas; evaluating and analysing ideas; analysing how reliable sources are; and identifying, explaining, and analysing historical interpretations.

Plenary suggestions

- Students could be referred to **Source A**, the monument to the Great Fire of London. They could be asked to come up with a new inscription, explaining the origin of the fire and why it spread so quickly.

Differentiation suggestions

Support

- In **Task 1**, lower ability students could be given a table with the sources to use for evidence already identified.

- In **Task 2**, lower ability students could be given summaries of the interpretation in each source and asked to simply put them in chronological order.

Extension: Hungry for more?

- Higher ability students could be asked to research how London changed immediately after the fire, as a prelude to the next lesson.

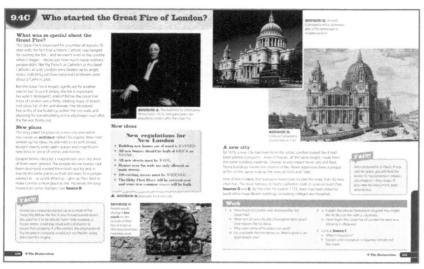

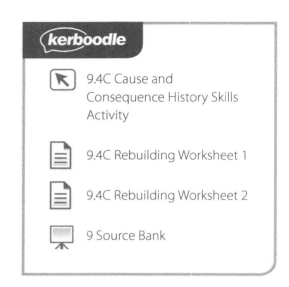

Renaissance, Revolution and Reformation pages 130–131

Lesson summary

Students will make a pitch to King Charles II about rebuilding a better London. This lesson includes a focus on numeracy (working within a budget).

What are the lesson outcomes?

All students will identify the problems with the poor housing in London prior to the Great Fire of London.

Most students will explain why interpretations of the Great Fire of London have changed over time.

Some students will explain why having to rebuild London was both a good thing and a bad thing.

Starter suggestion

- Students could be asked to list the problems with housing in London that helped the Great Fire to spread so quickly in 1666.

Main learning suggestions and assessment

What activities will take place?

Task 1: Before reading the information on pages 130–131, students could be set an activity in which they become part of the planning committee in charge of rebuilding London after the fire. They should be given some information about the problems with the old houses and the issues that need solving. Students should work in small groups to find a solution to each problem.

Task 2: Students should create a pitch to give to Charles II (you, the teacher) explaining how they will rebuild a better London. To turn this into a problem-solving activity, students could be given a budget and costs for each type of building. For example, a stone house could cost £100 and take six

months to build, while a wooden one could cost £50 and take just one month to build. Students' presentations could include drawings of plans or even 3D models.

Task 3: Students should read pages 130–131 and use the information to complete Work activities **1–3**.

Task 4: Students could complete 9.4C Rebuilding Worksheet 1, in which they create a tourist guide for the 'new and improved' London.

How will students demonstrate their understanding?
In **Tasks 1** and **2** students develop skills in teamwork and there are cross-curricular links to Maths (working within a budget) and English (speaking and listening skills).

Plenary suggestions

- Each group could be allocated another group to give feedback on during the pitches to Charles II. They should suggest at least one thing the group did well and give one piece of constructive criticism.

- Students could complete 9.4C Rebuilding Worksheet 2.

Differentiation suggestions

Support

- In **Task 1** lower ability students could complete a 'problems and solutions' table, in which the problems are already identified. Students need only think about possible solutions.

- In **Task 2** lower ability students should not be given a budget to work to. This will allow them to focus on their understanding of the historical skills and concepts.

Extension: Hungry for more?

- Students could complete 9.4C Cause and Consequence History Skills Activity.

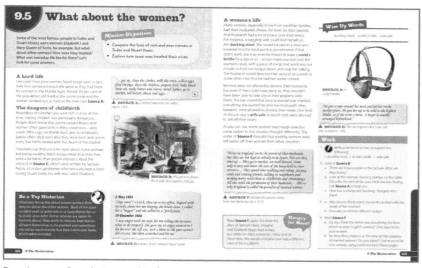

Renaissance, Revolution and Reformation pages 132–133

Lesson summary

Students will compare and contrast the lives of rich and poor women and explain how typical a source is.

What are the lesson outcomes?

All students will use empathy to describe the experiences of women living in this era.

Most students will use their own knowledge to put a source into its historical context.

Some students will analyse how typical a source is, using evidence from the source and their own knowledge.

Starter suggestion

- Students could make a list of the significant figures that they have studied so far in this period of history. Then they could make a pie chart to show how many of these people are male and how many are female. Ask them to make inferences about the lives of women at this time, based on their findings.

Main learning suggestions and assessment

What activities will take place?

Task 1: Students should read pages 132–133 and use the information to complete Work activities **1–4**.

Task 2: For each of the six sources on pages 132–133, students should draw the head of a woman with a 'thought bubble'. Inside each one they should write how they think the women that the source is concerned with might feel.

Task 3: Students should compare and contrast the lives of rich and poor women by completing a two-column table. They should highlight anything that would have been the same for both groups.

Task 4: Students should then focus on **Source F** and answer the question: 'Are you surprised by this source?' They should put it into its historical context to do this.

Task 5: Students should watch 9.5 Daily Life Film Clip and complete 9.5 Film Worksheet. They should then complete 9.5 Women Worksheet to consolidate their knowledge.

How will students demonstrate their understanding?

In **Task 2** students use empathy to describe the experiences of different groups of women. **Task 3** helps students to recall, identify, and describe ideas which they can then develop into a comparison between the lives of the rich and the poor. In **Task 4**, depending on the complexity of their answer, students will: identify ideas; use evidence from a source; use their own knowledge to put the source in its historical context; and/or analyse how typical the source is using their own knowledge.

Plenary suggestions

- Students could be given exemplar answers to the question they answered in **Task 4** and be asked to rank them from 'good' to 'best'.

Differentiation suggestions

Support

- In **Task 3** lower ability students could be given cards with descriptions of the lives of rich and poor women.

Extension: Hungry for more?

- Students could make inferences about the provenance of **Source A**. What can they infer from the fact that it was written by a man about his wife?

- Students could complete 9.5 Using Evidence History Skills Activity.

9.6 Can you cure King Charles II?

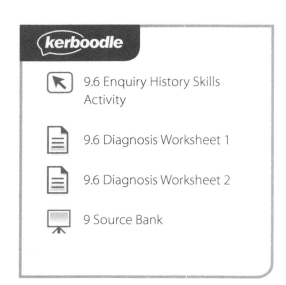

Renaissance, Revolution and Reformation pages 134–135

Lesson summary

Students will complete a decision-making exercise to work out how effective they would have been as a Renaissance doctor! This lesson includes cross-curricular links to Science and critical thinking.

What are the lesson outcomes?

All students will make decisions about how to treat Charles II.

Most students will use their prior knowledge of Renaissance medicine to make decisions about how to treat Charles II.

Some students will explain why Renaissance medicine was often quite bizarre!

Starter suggestion

- Students could create a list or a spider diagram of what they already know about medicine in this era. This will help them to make decisions later in the lesson.

Main learning suggestions and assessment

What activities will take place?

Task 1: Students should read pages 134–135 and complete the decision-making exercise. In this they must decide on the treatments to use to heal the king, then add up their score to see who is the best Renaissance doctor in the class! Both of the worksheets for this lesson support this task.

Task 2: Students should then complete Work activities **1–3** and 9.6 Enquiry History Skills Activity.

Task 3: Students should work in pairs to create an episode of a soap opera called 'King's Casualty' in which the king is treated by his doctors.

Task 4: Students should write an obituary for Charles II, in which they explain how he died (based on medical knowledge from the time). Inform students that obituaries sometimes start with the most important facts about the person, rather than being in chronological order.

How will students demonstrate their understanding?

In **Task 1**, students use their knowledge of Renaissance medicine to identify the most likely remedies doctors would have used. In Work activity **3**, they complete a piece of extended writing in which they identify, describe, and explain Renaissance medical practices.

Plenary suggestions

- Ask students to nominate Charles II for 'Man of the Match' by explaining why he was a good leader compared to the other Stuart rulers (James I, Charles I, and Cromwell). If they feel particularly strongly that he does not deserve this title, they could choose one of the other leaders and explain why they feel that they are more deserving.

Differentiation suggestions

Support

- It may be useful to provide calculators for lower ability students to help them tally their score in **Task 1**.

- Differentiation by support is possible in **Task 3**, by choosing suitable pairings rather than allowing students to select their own partner.

Extension: Hungry for more?

- In this lesson reference is made to Greek and Roman ideas about medicine that dominated in the seventeenth century. Students could research these in more detail including the 'four humours'.

Overview:
Chapter 10 Who rules?

Helping you deliver KS3 History National Curriculum

This chapter covers a lot of the example content from the KS3 History National Curriculum for 2014 – the 'Glorious Revolution' and power of Parliament; and the Act of Union of 1707, the Hanoverian succession and the Jacobite Rebellions of 1715 and 1745.

Each lesson in the chapter will encourage students to know about and understand these pivotal moments in British history. Students will also have the opportunity to put events in chronological order, recognize and describe change and continuity, identify causes and explain the relationships between them, and assess the significance of events, individuals, and ideas in both the short and long term.

The Big Picture

Why are we teaching 'Who rules?'?

The question of whether power resided with the Crown or Parliament could have been investigated in other chapters of this book, such as *Chapter 7 England at war*. However, we felt that a separate chapter on the causes, events, and consequences of the Glorious Revolution was the best place to cover this. We focus on the monumental transfer of power that occurred in the late seventeenth century, without the distraction of Civil War fighting and bloodshed!

The first lesson explores James II's accession to the throne. The students should be familiar with the hostility towards Catholicism that existed at the time, and they should be able to make connections to the religious seesawing in Tudor times. The next lesson covers the remarkable story of a

Skills and processes covered in this chapter

		10.1A	10.1B	10.2	10.3
History skills	Historical enquiry				✓
	Using evidence and source work		✓		✓
	Chronological understanding		✓	✓	
	Understanding cultural, ethnic and religious diversity	✓	✓	✓	
	Change and continuity	✓	✓	✓	
	Cause and consequence	✓	✓	✓	
	Significance		✓	✓	✓
	Interpretations				
	Making links/connections	✓	✓	✓	
	Explores similarities and differences			✓	
Literacy and numeracy	Key words identified/deployed		✓	✓	
	Extended writing				
	Encourages reading for meaning	✓	✓	✓	✓
	Focuses on structuring writing				
	Asks students to use writing to explore and develop ideas	✓	✓	✓	✓
	Learn through talk/discussion				
	Numeracy opportunities			✓	
Activity types	Creative task		✓		✓
	Emphasizes role of individual				✓
	Group work				
	Independent research	✓			
	Develops study skills			✓	

daughter removing her father from the throne, and the long-term consequences of an event that helped to shape Britain's constitutional monarchy and parliamentary democracy.

We then explore the establishment of the United Kingdom with the Act of Union during the time of Queen Anne. Finally there is a lesson on the Jacobite Rebellions and the Battle of Culloden, in part due to the latter's historical significance as the last battle to take place on British soil. The battle also represents the death rattle of the Stuart claim to the British throne, and brings the period to a logical, tidy conclusion.

Lesson sequence

Lesson title	NC references	Objectives	Outcomes	
10.1A The Glorious Revolution pp136–137 **10.1B The Glorious Revolution pp138–139**	'Glorious Revolution' and power of Parliament	• Recall the main events that led to the return of a Protestant monarchy. • Examine the reasons why the monarchy changed from Catholic to Protestant. • Evaluate the changes that William and Mary agreed to.	**All** students will explain what a turning point is, and give examples of turning points. **Most** students will decide and explain which of James II's actions were the most significant. **Some** students will analyse the significance of different turning points.	
10.2 Exit the Stuarts... enter the Georgians pp140–141	'Glorious Revolution' and power of Parliament The Act of Union of 1707 Hanoverian succession	• Investigate the consequences of the Glorious Revolution. • Explain the official establishment of the United Kingdom.	**All** students will categorize evidence to describe the establishment of the United Kingdom. **Most** students will explain the different methods used by monarchs to establish and rule the United Kingdom. **Some** students will analyse which was the most effective method used by monarchs to establish and rule the United Kingdom.	
10.3 The Battle of Culloden pp142–143	'Glorious Revolution' and power of Parliament Hanoverian succession Jacobite rebellions of 1715 and 1745	• Define the word 'Jacobite'. • Examine the Jacobite Rebellions of 1715 and 1745. • Explain why Bonnie Prince Charlie was a threat to the Georgians.	**All** students will identify evidence of bias within a source. **Most** students will annotate a source to explain its meaning. **Some** students will answer questions on the use and/or reliability of a source, using its historical context to explain any issues a historian using it might face.	

Ideas for enrichment

This chapter shares curriculum links with Citizenship – examining the role and powers of the monarch.

Students could carry out a research project on William of Orange and his legacy. This could involve his role in Holland, the Battle of the Boyne, the Orange Order of today and William's reign in England.

Culloden was the last great battle fought on British soil. Ask students to compile a 'Top Five' British battles… and you can bet Hastings will be number one!

You could ask students to write a biography of Bonnie Prince Charlie – he lived a rather fascinating (and controversial) life in exile!

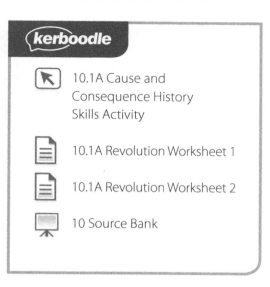

Renaissance, Revolution and Reformation pages 136–137

Lesson summary

Students will analyse the actions of James II by ranking them in order of how much they would have upset Parliament. They will then explain the significance of each action.

What are the lesson outcomes?

All students will explain what a turning point is, and give examples of turning points.

Most students will decide and explain which of James II's actions were the most significant.

Some students will analyse the significance of different turning points.

Starter suggestion

- Give students a list of Tudor and Stuart monarchs and ask them to write 'Catholic' or 'Protestant' next to each one. This will help to consolidate their prior learning about why religion was such a hot issue in this era.

Main learning suggestions and assessment

What activities will take place?

Task 1: Students should read pages 136–137 and use the information to complete Work activities **1–3**.

Task 2: Students should develop their answer to Work activity **3** by drawing a 'speech bubble' next to each of James II's actions explaining why it was significant.

Task 3: Students should compare and contrast James II with his father, Charles I, in order to decide whether James II's actions could have led to another civil war.

Task 4: Students should complete 10.1A Revolution Worksheets 1 and 2, which ask students to consider what effect James' reign had on his Protestant subjects.

Task 5: Students should complete 10.1A Cause and Consequence History Skills Activity, which involves assessing the importance of the causes of the Glorious Revolution.

How will students demonstrate their understanding?

In Work activity **3**, students start analysing the significance of James' actions by ranking them in order. **Task 2** develops this further, by asking students to explain the significance of each action. In **Task 3** students place events into their historical context when comparing and contrasting James with his father.

Plenary suggestions

- Ask students to imagine being a Member of Parliament. They have to come up with an action plan to solve the potential problems that James II is causing.

Differentiation suggestions

Support

- In Work activity **3**, students could work in small groups to discuss the significance of each of James' actions. Each action could be written on a card so that students can move them around, making the activity kinaesthetic and allowing students to change their minds more easily.

- In **Task 2** lower ability students could be given a set of 'speech bubbles', with Parliament's concerns already written in, so they can match pairs.

Extension: Hungry for more?

- Students could complete the 'Hungry for More?' activity on page 137. In this they need to find out why James II's new son is often called the 'warming pan baby'. They could use their research to write a headline or article for a sensationalist tabloid newspaper.

10.1B The Glorious Revolution

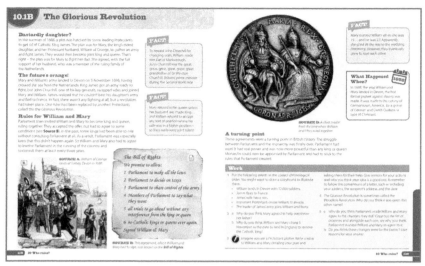

Renaissance, Revolution and Reformation pages 138–139

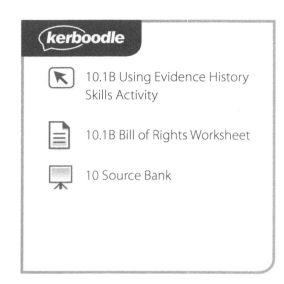

Lesson summary

Students will consider what constitutes a 'turning point' and analyse the Bill of Rights..

What are the lesson outcomes?

All students will explain what a turning point is, and give examples of turning points.

Most students will decide and explain which of James II's actions were the most significant.

Some students will analyse the significance of different turning points.

Starter suggestion

- Give students a list of Tudor and Stuart monarchs and ask them to use the mathematical symbols for inequalities ('greater than' and 'less than', or 'hungry crocodiles'!) to write equations showing who they think was most powerful during each reign – the monarch or Parliament. For example:
  - Elizabeth I > Parliament

Main learning suggestions and assessment

What activities will take place?

Task 1: Students should read pages 138–139 and use the information to complete Work activities **1–5**.

Task 2: Ask students to write a paragraph explaining what a turning point is, using an example from the events of the Glorious Revolution to explain the term.

Task 3: Students should copy out each of the promises made by William and Mary (**Source B**). Ask students to colour-code them to show which are still followed by the monarch and Parliament today. They could then write a paragraph explaining the significance of the Bill of Rights.

Task 4: Students could be shown an image of a dual-headed coin, minted during the reign of William and Mary. Ask students to pretend that they are curators for the Royal Mint Museum. They have been asked to produce an exhibition in which this coin is displayed, and must create a plaque explaining why the coin is so different from others on display.

How will students demonstrate their understanding?

In **Task 2,** students define, identify, describe, and/or explain the term 'turning point'. In **Task 3**, students describe, explain, and/or analyse the significance of the Bill of Rights.

Plenary suggestions

- In the plenary of *8.4B Whatever happened to Cromwell's head?* students considered the meaning of the word 'revolution' in relation to the Restoration, deciding whether it was 'a sudden and violent change to power' or 'travelling a full circle to return to where you started – like the revolution of a wheel'. In this lesson students could be asked which definition they would use for the Glorious Revolution. This enables students to consider which revolution was the more significant, and why.

Differentiation suggestions

Support

- In **Task 2**, it may be necessary to recap how to write a PEE (point, evidence, explanation) paragraph with lower ability students.

Extension: Hungry for more?

- Students could complete 10.1B Using Evidence History Skills Activity or 10.1B Bill of Rights Worksheet, perhaps as homework.

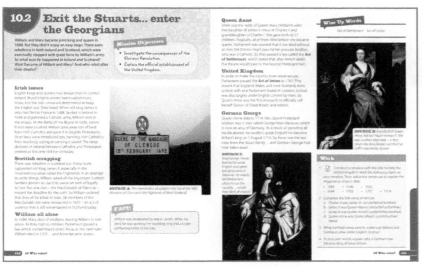

Renaissance, Revolution and Reformation pages 140–141

Lesson summary

Students will categorize evidence into a Venn diagram, in order to plan and write an essay about the methods of control used to establish and rule the United Kingdom. This lesson includes cross-curricular links to English (writing an argumentative essay) and Mathematics (using a Venn diagram to represent data).

What are the lesson outcomes?

All students will categorize evidence to describe the establishment of the United Kingdom.

Most students will explain the different methods used by monarchs to establish and rule the United Kingdom.

Some students will analyse which was the most effective method used by monarchs to establish and rule the United Kingdom.

Starter suggestion

- Show students a Union Jack, and ask them to annotate it to show what they think the different lines and colours represent.

Main learning suggestions and assessment

What activities will take place?

Task 1: Students should read pages 140–141 and use the information to complete Work activities **1–4**.

Task 2: Students should write a speech for a general to give his men, shortly before the Battle of the Boyne, explaining what they are fighting for.

Task 3: Students should create a Venn diagram in which they consider the different methods used to control England, Ireland, and Scotland. The categories should be: 'Violence'; 'Laws'; and 'Tradition'. Tradition could relate to the passing of the crown down the royal line.

Task 4: Students should write an essay entitled 'What was the most effective method that monarchs used to unite and rule the United Kingdom?' They could then self- or peer-assess their work.

Task 5: Students should complete 10.2 Understanding Diversity History Skills Activity. They should also complete 10.2 Timeline Worksheet, in which they identify the key events in the formation of the United Kingdom and put them in chronological order.

How will students demonstrate their understanding?

Tasks 1 and **2** test students' comprehension of the content of this lesson. **Task 3** enables students to categorize evidence so that they can use this to present and explain the different methods in their essay. In **Task 4** students are able to demonstrate their ability to identify, describe, explain, and/or analyse the different methods of control.

Plenary suggestions

- Students could analyse the consequences of the Glorious Revolution by 'hot seating' different characters, asking relevant questions, and answering to show their understanding.

Differentiation suggestions

Support

- In **Task 3** lower ability students could be given evidence cards to sort into their Venn diagram, while other students could identify their own.

- In **Task 4** lower ability students could use a writing frame complete with sentence starters.

Extension: Hungry for more?

- Students could research and create a royal family tree, showing how the Stuart and Georgian monarchs were related, and following the royal line down to today.

10.3 The Battle of Culloden

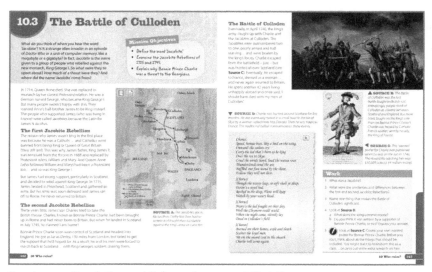

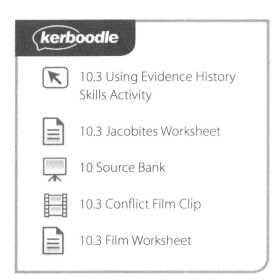

Renaissance, Revolution and Reformation pages 142–143

Lesson summary

Students will analyse *The Skye Boat Song* using their contextual knowledge of the Jacobite Rebellions. This lesson includes cross-curricular links to English (analysing a poem/ballad).

What are the lesson outcomes?

All students will identify evidence of bias within a source.

Most students will annotate a source to explain its meaning.

Some students will answer questions on the use and/or reliability of a source, using its historical context to explain any issues a historian using it might face.

Starter suggestion

- Play students a version of *The Skye Boat Song* (**Source D**) and ask them to work out what they think it is about.

Main learning suggestions and assessment

What activities will take place?

Task 1: Students should read pages 142–143 and use the information to complete Work activities **1–5**. For Work activity **4**, give students a copy of **Source D**. Ask them to find evidence to prove whose side the ballad is on, by highlighting words that are biased.

Task 2: Students should watch 10.3 Conflict Film Clip and complete 10.3 Film Worksheet

Task 3: Students should complete a source analysis of **Source D**. They could be asked: what its meaning is; what interpretation of Bonnie Prince Charlie it gives; how useful it is to a historian studying the second Jacobite Rebellion; how reliable it is.

Task 4: Students should complete 10.3 Using Evidence History Skills Activity. In this they focus on different aspects of **Source D**, so this activity consolidates the skills developed in **Tasks 2** and **3**. They should then complete 10.3 Jacobites Worksheet.

How will students demonstrate their understanding?

This lesson tests students' abilities to use evidence from a source; put it in its historical context; analyse how useful it is; or analyse its reliability.

Plenary suggestions

- Students could demonstrate and consolidate the source analysis skills they have developed this lesson by analysing the use and reliability of **Source B**.

Differentiation suggestions

Support

- In **Task 1** lower ability students could be provided with a key words dictionary to help their comprehension of the ballad.

- In **Task 3** there are four questions that can be selected. Students could do all four, an appropriate selection, or just one.

- For work activity **5**, you might like to hold a brief class discussion on the features of a 'Wanted' poster before starting the task.

Extension: Hungry for more?

- In 2011 the law changed so that a member of the royal family can now marry a Catholic. Students could research this change. They could try to work out if the rule that the monarch cannot be Catholic (from the Bill of Rights, 1689) is still in force today.

Overview:
Chapter 11 How did Britain change?

Helping you deliver KS3 History National Curriculum

This concluding chapter challenges students to evaluate the historical concepts of change and continuity, cause and consequence, and similarity and difference. The impact of new ideas, discoveries, and inventions – both in Britain and the wider world – are covered here. Significant events (such as the founding of The Royal Society) and key ideas (such as Francis Bacon's use of the 'Scientific Method') are examined in this chapter. Students will discover how people's lives (including their own) have been shaped by some of these ideas, inventions, and discoveries. They will be required to recognize that some events, people, and changes might be judged as more important than others. They will be asked to make use of appropriate historical terminology to produce structured work.

The Big Picture

Why are we teaching 'How did Britain change?'?

The final chapter of the book is intended to get students to think deeply about the process of change. In the first lesson, students are introduced to 'John', a character from early Tudor times. Some might even recall him from the previous book, *Invasion, Plague and Murder*! They are asked to consider what John knows (or thinks he knows) about some aspects of the world he lives in. The character talks about his beliefs about the world, health and medicine, the universe, and so on.

After establishing what the typical mind-set of an early Tudor might be, students are taken on a journey through the early years of the Age of Enlightenment, covering many key scientific, philosophical, architectural, and medical developments. Students are then introduced to 'Robert',

Skills and processes covered in this chapter

		11.1A	11.1B	11.2A	11.2B
History skills	Historical enquiry	✓	✓	✓	✓
	Using evidence and source work			✓	✓
	Chronological understanding	✓	✓	✓	✓
	Understanding cultural, ethnic and religious diversity	✓	✓	✓	✓
	Change and continuity	✓	✓	✓	✓
	Cause and consequence			✓	✓
	Significance			✓	✓
	Interpretations				
	Making links/connections	✓	✓	✓	✓
	Explores similarities and differences	✓	✓	✓	✓
Literacy and numeracy	Key words identified/deployed				✓
	Extended writing		✓		✓
	Encourages reading for meaning	✓	✓	✓	✓
	Focuses on structuring writing				
	Asks students to use writing to explore and develop ideas		✓		✓
	Learn through talk/discussion	✓			✓
	Numeracy opportunities	✓			
Activity types	Creative task		✓		
	Emphasizes role of individual			✓	✓
	Group work				
	Independent research				
	Develops study skills		✓		✓

a Georgian gentleman from the mid-1700s. Dotted around Robert are some questions that ask students to think hard about change – and the causes of change. Hopefully, by giving a human face (or faces) to the Tudor and Georgian period, and introducing students to the way people might have thought, we can help students more easily understand the concepts of continuity and change.

The final lesson of the chapter takes a broad, overview approach to various aspects of British life, such as population, transport, law and order, and communication. It takes a snapshot of each aspect in three different years (1509,1603 and 1745). The intention here is to reinforce the chronological framework of the book, enable the students to revisit previous learning, and help them gain an insight into the extent and speed of change that took place between 1509 and 1745.

Lesson sequence

Lesson title	NC references	Objectives	Outcomes
11.1A What does Robert know that John didn't? pp144–145 **11.1B What does Robert know that John didn't?** pp146–147	Society, economy and culture across the period	• Examine the difference between the Age of Faith and the Age of Reason. • Explore some of the key discoveries, theories and inventions of the sixteenth, seventeenth and early eighteenth centuries.	**All** students will identify significant individuals, events, and developments in order to demonstrate their understanding of the era. **Most** students will make connections and draw contrasts across the era. **Some** students will analyse trends within periods and over long arcs of time
11.2A A changing nation pp148–149 **11.2B A changing nation** pp150–151	Society, economy and culture across the period	• Judge how far Britain changed between 1509 and 1745. • Recall at least five important ideas and inventions that came from this time.	**All** students will summarize trends across the Tudor and Stuart eras. **Most** students will match developments to their causes. **Some** students will explain the significance of events by analysing cause and consequence.
Assessing Your Learning 3: Why should we remember them? pp152–153	Dependent on person being researched	• Research a chosen individual. • Judge the individual's historical significance.	**All** students will identify an individual and explain their importance. **Most** students will accurately describe a chosen person's significance using the correct historical terms. **Some** students will outline the significant contribution of their chosen individual in both the short and long term, and will identify the sources they have used.

Ideas for enrichment

This chapter can form the basis of an excellent end of year classroom display. You can designate different areas of life (power, population, religion and so on) to different groups and ask them to illustrate the changes on one A3 (or A2) sheet of paper. This can take the form of graphs to show populations, posters to illustrate leisure pursuits, maps to illustrate the extent of the known world, and so on.

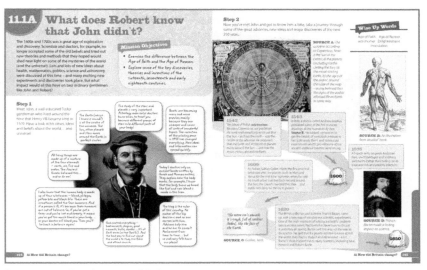

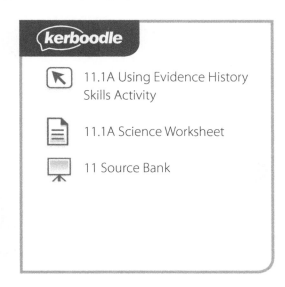

Renaissance, Revolution and Reformation pages 144–145

Lesson summary

Students will compare and contrast the lives of people living at the start of the Tudor era with those of people living at the end of the Stuart era, in order to develop chronological understanding.

What are the lesson outcomes?

All students will identify significant individuals, events, and developments in order to demonstrate their understanding of the era.

Most students will make connections and draw contrasts across the era.

Some students will analyse trends within periods and over long arcs of time.

Starter suggestion

- Students could select the contents for a 'time capsule' for the era, using their knowledge to decide which items best represent the key characteristics, individuals, and changes.

Main learning suggestions and assessment

What activities will take place?

Task 1: Students should read the information on page 144 and then create a comparison table, which they will complete over this lesson and the next. In this table they should summarize John's beliefs and knowledge.

Task 2: Students should use the timeline on page 145 to create fact files for two of the significant individuals mentioned. See page 84 in the *Student Book* for an example of a fact file. Alternatively, they could complete 11.1A Science Worksheet, which focuses on the developments or inventions themselves.

Task 3: Students should complete 11.1A Using Evidence History Skills Activity.

How will students demonstrate their understanding?

Students will develop skills that allow them to identify, describe, explain, evaluate, and analyse significant events, individuals, and developments within the Tudor and Stuart eras. This lesson consolidates knowledge from throughout the *Student Book*.

Plenary suggestions

- Students could reconsider the contents of their 'time capsule' from the starter activity. By swapping their work with a partner, peer-assessment can be used to work out whether anything should be added or removed.

Differentiation suggestions

Support

- In **Task 1** lower ability students could be given typed facts that can be stuck into the comparison table, rather than having to create their own summaries.

Extension: Hungry for more?

- One of the significant individuals considered in this lesson is Galileo. Students could research the play *Life of Galileo* by Bertolt Brecht to give them an idea of the context in which Galileo developed his ideas. For students who go on to study Germany in the early twentieth century, Brecht is an example of a Weimar playwright who fled Germany when the Nazis came into power. For students who study America in the twentieth century, Brecht is an example of a playwright blacklisted by Hollywood because of his Marxist beliefs.

- Alternatively, students could add a column for a medieval person on their comparison table. This will help students to achieve the outcome of analysing trends within periods and across long arcs of time.

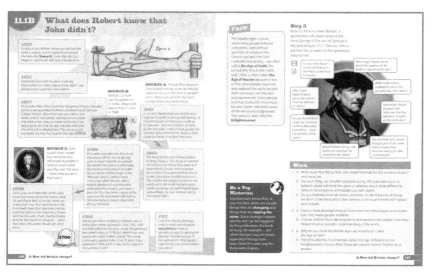

Renaissance, Revolution and Reformation pages 146–147

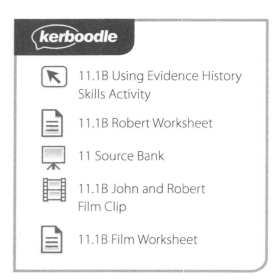

Lesson summary

Students will compare and contrast the lives of people living at the start of the Tudor era with those of people living at the end of the Stuart era, in order to develop chronological understanding.

What are the lesson outcomes?

All students will identify significant individuals, events, and developments in order to demonstrate their understanding of the era.

Most students will make connections and draw contrasts across the era.

Some students will analyse trends within periods and over long arcs of time.

Starter suggestion

● To consolidate their knowledge of developments in the sixteenth and early seventeenth century, students could be asked to recreate the timeline they studied by placing events into the correct chronological order.

Main learning suggestions and assessment

What activities will take place?

Task 1: Students should read pages 146–147 and use the information to complete Work activities **1–3** and 11.1B Robert Worksheet.

Task 2: Students should watch 11.1A John and Robert Film Clip and complete 11.1A Film Worksheet.

Task 3: Students should create a composite picture, summarizing the world and universe as John understands it. They should do this by drawing the outline of a man and then adding features that represent his ideas, beliefs, understanding, and knowledge. For example, his jacket could be decorated with a heart pattern to represent that William

Harvey proved that the heart is a pump that circulates blood. Students should then swap their work with a partner who must annotate the picture to explain what has been included and why.

Task 4: Students should complete the comparison table they started last lesson by summarising Robert's beliefs and knowledge.

Task 5: In the 'Robert' column of their comparison table, students should colour-code each row in order to indicate whether it shows progress, stagnation, or regression of knowledge and understanding across the era.

How will students demonstrate their understanding?

In this lesson, students identify changes and trends, make connections, draw contrasts, and analyse trends within the periods studied.

Plenary suggestions

● Ask students why they think the era is often known as 'the Age of Reason' or 'the Enlightenment'.

Differentiation suggestions

Support

● In **Task 3** lower ability students could be given a list of developments that they need to include in their picture.

● In **Task 4** lower ability students could focus on one category, which they feed back to the rest of the class on.

Extension: Hungry for more?

● Students could complete 11.1B Using Evidence History Skills Activity, in which they analyse **Source B**. The final activity could be developed further, designing a bank note featuring a significant individual from the sixteenth, seventeenth or eighteenth century, and then writing a letter to the Royal Mint explaining why this design should be adopted.

11.2A A changing nation

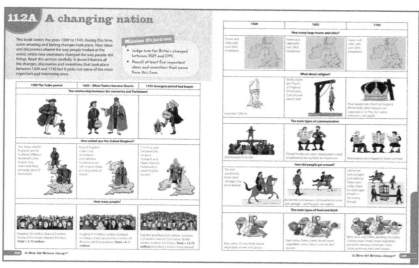

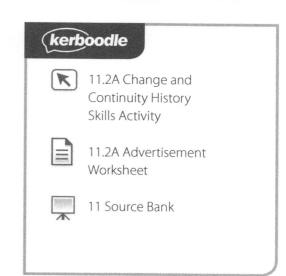

Renaissance, Revolution and Reformation pages 148–149

Lesson summary

Students will match trends within periods to the events that caused them. This lesson includes a focus on numeracy (statistical analysis and analysing positive and negative relationships).

What are the lesson outcomes?

All students will summarize trends across the Tudor and Stuart eras.

Most students will match developments to their causes.

Some students will explain the significance of events by analysing cause and consequence.

Starter suggestion

- Complete 11.2A Change and Continuity History Skills Activity with the class to assess their confidence with the predominant skill for this lesson.

Main learning suggestions and assessment

What activities will take place?

Task 1: Students should read pages 148–149 and use the information to create a table in which they first describe the trend for each category. For example:

Category	Description of trend	Cause(s)
The relationship between the monarchy and Parliament		

Task 2: Students should then complete the 'Cause(s)' column in the above table.

Task 3: Students should write a PEE (point, evidence, explanation) paragraph, explaining which change they think was the most significant/important and why.

How will students demonstrate their understanding?

In **Task 1**, students will summarize and describe trends. In **Task 2** most students will match causes to their consequences. In **Task 4**, students will analyse the significance of different causes and consequences.

Plenary suggestions

- Provide a number of key words/phrases from the lesson or chapter. Students should come to the front to 'draw' their word or phrase. The class must guess what the word or phrase is.

Differentiation suggestions

Support

- In **Task 1** lower ability students could each take one category to focus on and research. Each student could then feed back their ideas back to the group.

- In **Task 4** lower ability students could be provided with a writing frame that includes sentence starters.

Extension: Hungry for more?

- Students could consider the ideas of change, progression, and regression by analysing each development and deciding whether, in the long term, it was a positive or negative development.

- Students could complete 11.2A Advertisement Worksheet as homework.

11.2B A changing nation

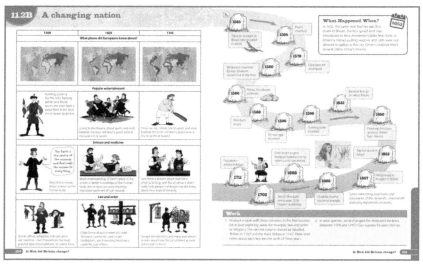

Renaissance, Revolution and Reformation pages 150–151

Lesson summary
Students will match trends within periods to the events that caused them. This lesson includes a focus on numeracy (statistical analysis and analysing positive and negative relationships).

What are the lesson outcomes?
All students will summarize trends across the Tudor and Stuart eras.

Most students will match developments to their causes.

Some students will explain the significance of events by analysing cause and consequence.

Starter suggestion
- Students could complete a 'linking lines' activity to match causes to their consequences, such as Charles I dismissing Parliament linking to the English Civil War.

Main learning suggestions and assessment
What activities will take place?
Task 1: Students should read pages 150–151 and use the information to complete Work activities **1–2** and 11.2B Changing Britain Worksheet.

Task 2: Students should create 'evolution' diagrams to summarize the changes shown in one area. They may have seen the 'evolution of man' diagram, in which ape evolves into man. Their work should be based on this. So for example, for 'types of food and drink' students could show a human whose waistline expands and who becomes tidier after a meal, to represent the increase in types of food available and the use of cutlery. They should label and explain their diagrams.

Task 3: Ask students to create their own revision booklet, which summarizes the changes in each area studied across pages 148–151. They could use this to prepare for *Assessing Your Learning 3*.

Task 4: Hold a class debate on which changes had the biggest impact.

Task 5: Students should analyse whether any of the trends link to each other. For example, the increased availability of books, newspapers, and magazines could link to better understanding of science and medicine. This activity could take the form of a flow diagram , for example. However, higher ability students might prefer to write an essay about the developments.

How will students demonstrate their understanding?
In Work activity **2**, students demonstrate their ability to analyse how significant a development or trend is. In **Task 5** students examine how causes, consequences, and trends are often interlinked. This enables them to analyse the significance of different developments by looking at which were catalysts for big changes across many aspects of life, and which had much narrower consequences.

Plenary suggestions
- You could complete 11.2B Significance History Skills Activity, a fun mini quiz, as a class.

Differentiation suggestions
Support
- In **Task 2** lower ability students could focus on one aspect or development.

Extension: Hungry for more?
- Students could be encouraged to examine trends over a long arc of time. To do this they could create their own diagrams, similar to those on pages 148–150, but with just two boxes: 1745 and today.

Assessing Your Learning 3

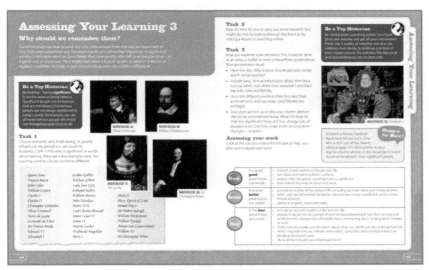

Renaissance, Revolution and Reformation pages 152–153

Renaissance, Revolution and Reformation pages 152–153

Student Book
- Assessment task
- Student 'Assessing your work' grid

kerboodle

Assessment Task Presentation 3

Assessment Worksheet 3

Success Criteria Teacher Grid 3

Teacher Handbook
- Success Criteria Teacher Grid 3

Assessment in the *Student Book*

In this assessment task, students are asked to analyse the significance of key individuals from the eras studied. They present their work in the form of a presentation.

The ability to consider the significance of people and developments in their historical context and in the present day is a skill that students should develop at Key Stage 3, according to the National Curriculum for 2014. This assessment also allows students to develop their ability to conduct historical enquiries.

In the *Student Book* (and on the supporting worksheets) you'll find guidance of success criteria that you can use to help your students understand what their work should include. You could ask them to use this criteria for self- or peer-assessment once they have completed the task.

Chapter 11 How did Britain change? assessment task

Task 1:
Choose someone who lived during the period you are currently studying (1509–1745) who is significant or worth remembering. There are a few examples on page 152 of the *Student Book*, but you may want to choose someone different.

Task 2:
Now it's time for you to carry out some research. You might do that by looking through the *Student Book*, visiting a library, or searching online.

Task 3:
Now put together a presentation. This could be done as an essay, a leaflet or even a PowerPoint presentation.

Assessing your work

In a **good** presentation, you would…	• provide a basic outline of the person's life • use dates and historical terms correctly • explain why the person was important or significant. • begin to produce structured work.
In a **better** presentation, you would…	• provide an outline of the person's life, including accurate dates and historical terms • select and use information to explain why the person was significant, using correct historical terms • produce properly structured work.
In the **best** presentation, you would…	• provide an accurate outline of the person's life • explain in detail why the person should be remembered and how their actions and/or achievements changed lots of people's lives, mentioning short- or long-term changes, or both • show how you made your decisions about what was significant about the person's life • select, organize and use relevant information, using the correct historical terms to produce structured work • show where you got your information from.

Hungry for More?

Research a famous historical figure from this period in time who is NOT one of choices listed on page 152 of the *Student Book*. Write a letter to your teacher arguing why he or she should be included as one of the period's most significant people.

Success criteria teacher grid

Assessment criteria	Beginning/ Developing	Securing	Extending
	Current NC Level 3/4	Current NC Level 5/6	Current NC Level 7/8
	GCSE Grade Indicator E/D	GCSE Grade Indicator C/B	GCSE Grade Indicator A/A*
Remembering	Student can list three facts about their chosen person	Student can describe in detail five facts about the person they have chosen to research	
Understanding	Student can provide a basic outline of their person's life	Student can provide a basic outline of their person's life, including accurate dates and historical terms	Student can give a detailed outline of their person's life, based on a wide range of independent research
Applying	Student can select some important events or achievements in their chosen person's life	Student can explain the impact of their chosen person's achievements or events they were involved in	Student can select a number of events or achievements in their chosen person's life and explain why they made an impact
Analyzing	Student can identify why their chosen person is remembered	Student can explain the importance of the person they have researched in their particular field	Student can explain in detail why the person should be remembered and how their actions, inventions etc. changed people's lives
Evaluating	Student can justify why their chosen person was important or significant	Student can select and use information to explain why their person was significant, using proper historical terms	Student can explain why they believe their chosen person was significant in their particular field, and assess the short- and long-term impact they had
Creating	Student attempts to use the correct historical terminology and their answer is structured appropriately	Student selects, organizes and uses relevant information, including the correct historical terms, to produce a well-structured piece of work	Student selects, organizes and independently researches a wide range of relevant information and uses the correct historical terms to produce a well-structured piece of work

Glossary

Act of Settlement An act passed by Parliament stating that after Queen Anne's death the throne would pass to the nearest Protestant heir

Act of Union An act passed by Parliament to unite England, Scotland and Wales under the control of one parliament, based in London

Age of Faith The Middle Ages, when most people believed unquestioningly in the Church and God

Age of Reason Also known as the Enlightenment, the period during the 1600s and 1700s when people began to explore the world more and make new discoveries

Ally A group on the same side as another in battle

Antibiotic A chemical substance used to destroy bacteria

Anti-Stratfordian Someone who doubts that Shakespeare really wrote the plays attributed to him

Architect A designer of buildings

Armada A fleet of warships

Astrolabe A piece of navigation equipment that helped sailors work out how far north or south they were whilst at sea

Astronomer A person who scientifically studies stars, planets and other bodies of the universe

Beacon A fire set in a high place as a warning or signal

Belladonna A chemical used by Tudor women to make their eyes shine and sparkle

Bias To be for or against a person or group of people, especially in a way that is considered unfair

Bill of Mortality A weekly list of the causes of death in a particular place

Bill of Rights The agreements made between William and Mary and Parliament in 1689

Birch A bundle of twigs tied together and used to hit children as a punishment; a cane was a single piece of wood

Blood sports Sports that involve the wounding or killing of animals

Bloodletting The practice of making someone bleed to cure an illness

Bubonic A type of plague that causes huge, round boils or 'buboes'; carried by fleas

Canting A secretive street language used by sturdy beggars

Catholic A follower of Catholicism, one of the main Christian religions

Cavalier Nickname for a soldier who fought for the king during the English Civil War

Cavalry Soldiers on horseback

Citizen A person who lives in a town

Civil war A war between two groups of people in the same country

Class A group of people with the same economic or social status

Cochineal A red dye or colouring obtained from insects

Colony An area of land in a new country occupied by people who still remain under the rule of their homeland

Commonwealth An independent state or community without a monarch

Consummate To make a marriage legally recognised by having sex

Contemporary Something from the same period of time

Crescent A curved, moon-like shape

Cuckold The name for a married person whose husband or wife was having affairs behind their back

Cudgels A game for two people; each person has a heavy stick and they take it in turns to hit each other; the person left standing is the winner

Death warrant A piece of paper ordering someone's execution

Desolation Complete emptiness or destruction

Dissolution The act of officially breaking up an organization; used to describe the time when Henry VIII closed all the monasteries in England and Wales

Divine Right of Kings The belief that kings and queens could do as they wished because they were appointed by God

Ducking stool A punishment for 'unruly' wives

Enlightenment See **Age of Reason**

Excommunicate To expel from the Catholic Church; a very serious punishment

Execution The process of killing or beheading an enemy or convicted criminal

Extremist A supporter of extreme measures (often political or religious)

Familiar A demon, in the form of an animal, that accompanies a witch

Fire mark Displayed on the outside of people's houses to prove that their insurance fees had been paid

Forbade When someone has not allowed something to happen

Galleon A large warship

Gallery A place to sit in a theatre

Gangrene The death of tissues in the body caused by an infection or obstruction of blood flow

Gentleman Rich men, often dukes, earls or lords; they often own a lot of land

Grammar school A school that taught mainly Latin and Greek grammar

Gun-port An opening in a ship through which a gun can be fired

Heathen A person who has no religion or whose religion is not the same as that of another group of people

Hornbook A flat, double-sided paddle, shaped like a table-tennis bat; used to help students read and write

House of Correction Criminals and people who refused to work were sent here; they were forced to make things that were later sold

Imported Brought in from another country, usually by boat

Independent Free from the control of someone or something

Indulgences You could 'buy' these from a bishop; they helped a person pass through purgatory more quickly

Infantry Soldiers on foot

Infidel See **Heathen**

Inoculation A way of preventing a person getting a disease by introducing a small amount of it into their body, making them immune to it

Interregnum The period from the execution of Charles I in 1649 to when Charles II became king; when Oliver Cromwell ruled as Lord Protector

Labourer A person who does manual work such as working in the fields

Laxative A medicine used to help a person go to the toilet easily

Lord Protector The title of the head of state in England between 1653 and 1659, a position first held by Oliver Cromwell

Major-General A man appointed by Cromwell to run one of the 11 districts in England

Malaria A disease spread by mosquitoes

Martyr A person who is prepared to die for their beliefs

Merchant A person whose job is to buy and sell goods in order to make a profit

Mercy Showing understanding or kindness, especially to your enemy

Miscarry When a baby dies while it is still in the womb

Monarch A king or queen

Musket A type of long gun

Musketeer A soldier who carries a musket

Native American The tribesmen who have lived on the continent of North America for thousands of years

Native A member of the original race of a country; a person who was born in that country

Navigation The process of working out where you are

Obituary Briefly tells of some of the most important events, achievements and personality of a person who has recently died

Parliamentarian A supporter of Parliament during the English Civil War

Pauper Someone with no job who relies on charity

Pike A long pole, tipped with a steel spike; used as a weapon

Pikeman A soldier who uses a pike

Pilgrim A person who travels to a place for religious reasons; the first people to colonize America

Pirate A person who attacks and robs ships at sea

Pit The standing area nearest the stage in a theatre

Playwright A person who writes plays

Plundering Taking goods by force

Poor Law A law passed in 1601 that placed paupers into four categories; each group was treated differently

Pope The leader of the Catholic Church, who lives in Rome

Population All the people who live in a particular place

Privateer A sailor who had permission to attack and steal from foreign ships

Propaganda False or misleading information used to spread a certain point of view

Protestants A group of Christians who protested against the Catholic Church

Purgatory The place between heaven and hell; a person is believed to be punished in purgatory for any sins they have committed while alive

Quarter Mercy shown towards an enemy

Quill pen A pen made from a feather; dipped in ink to write

Recusant A Catholic who refused to accept the authority of the Church of England

Reformation The name used to describe the changes or reforms made to the Catholic Church in the sixteenth century, mainly by Henry VIII and his son, King Edward VI

Regicide The official word for killing a king or queen, or for someone who kills a king or queen

Religious Settlement Made by Elizabeth in order to keep the peace between Catholics and Protestants

Renaissance The period between the fourteenth and sixteenth centuries in Europe when there was a rebirth in art, literature and learning

Republic A country without a king or a queen

Restoration The return of a monarch to the throne of England when Charles II became king in 1660

Revolution The overthrowing of a government or social order in favour of a new system

Ridicule To make fun of someone in an unkind way

Roundhead Nickname for Parliament's soldiers during the English Civil War

Routine An established pattern of behaviour that people follow most of the time

Royalist A supporter of the king during the English Civil War

Sash A coloured strip of cloth used to identify soldiers in battle

Scold's bridle An iron mask put over a woman's head to stop her talking; used as a punishment

Searcher Someone who looked for the dead bodies of plague victims during the Great Plague of 1665

Settler Somebody who moved to an area that was previously uninhabited or unknown

Sewer A drain to remove waste water and other rubbish

Shin-hacking A game for two people; each person wears their heaviest boots, they take it in turns to kick each other, and the person left standing is the winner

Ship tax A sum of money, introduced by Charles I, paid by people who were living by the sea

Shorthand A type of coded writing that can be written quickly

Siege A method of attack where an army surrounds a town and threatens to attack unless the town surrenders

Slave A person who is the legal property of someone else and is forced to obey them

Slave trader A person who deals in the transporting and selling of human beings as slaves

Sphere Ball-shaped

Stillborn A baby that is born dead

Stratfordian Someone who believes that Shakespeare was responsible for writing the plays attributed to him

Strolling player A travelling actor, musician and entertainer

Sturdy beggar A criminal who used clever tricks to get money

Superstitious Someone who believes in omens and ghosts

Symptom A sign of an illness or disease

Tithe A type of tax; peasants had to give 10 per cent of their harvest to the priest every year

Treason A crime against a king or queen

Tuberculosis A lung disease

Tyrant A cruel and demanding ruler

Unstable Something that is not secure

Vagabonds Wanderers or tramps

Voyage A journey, usually by sea

Whitsun The seventh Sunday after Easter, also called Pentecost

Wife sale A type of divorce; in Tudor and Stuart England it was possible to sell your wife at one of these

Yeoman A farmer – some were rich; others were poor

Yield Surrender